Ray Wilkinson MA

Brodie's Notes on

A Choice of
Milton's Verse

Pan Educational London and Sydney

First published 1977 by Pan Books Ltd,
Cavaye Place, London SW10 9PG
1 2 3 4 5 6 7 8 9
© Ray Wilkinson 1977
ISBN 0 330 50098 8
Printed and bound in Great Britain by
Richard Clay (The Chaucer Press) Ltd, Bungay, Suffolk

Page references in these Notes are to the Faber edition
of *A Choice of Milton's Verse*, selected by D. J. Enright;
but references are usually given to particular parts and
chapters, so that the Notes may be used with any
edition of the book.

Contents

Milton's life

Milton was born in 1608. His father, who had been disinherited for deserting the family's Catholic religion, was a scrivener – a scribe or copyist – whose hobby and dominating interest was music. From his earliest years, Milton was an omnivorous reader. He attended St Paul's School and his studies were supplemented by a private tutor who taught him Hebrew, French and Italian to add to the Latin and Greek which were, of course, the staple of Renaissance education. He learned to compose Latin verse, to think in Latin. He wrote Latin verse for much of his life and often reserved his most personal thoughts for that language. There was still a European audience for Latin poems, and if a poet was looking for worldwide fame he might be ill-advised to write in English. Even while Milton was still a child, he and his father seem to have believed that he was chosen for some great work in learning and literature.

In 1625, shortly before the accession of Charles I, Milton went up to Christ's College, Cambridge. He seems to have been at odds with the authorities – a characteristic which remained with him for much of his life. He objected to the still-practised medieval system of education, based on disputation and scholastic logic, which Milton thought of as quibbling. But his work shows his own outstanding ability to argue a case, even a case in which he did not believe; for instance, in his portrayal of Satan and Comus. He came to distrust the art of rhetoric, which could easily degenerate into the art of lying convincingly. Possibly because of his youthful appearance and a certain fastidiousness, he was known as 'the lady of Christ's'. He wrote copiously at this time, both in Latin and in English, the English poems including some assured Elegies written before he was eighteen.

The *Nativity Ode* was written in 1629, when Milton was

twenty-one. He experimented with different forms and languages, writing some poems in Italian. He took his MA degree in 1632 and then went to his father's estate at Horton in Buckinghamshire where he stayed for six years, studying and continuing to prepare himself for his vocation as a poet. Here he wrote *At a Solemn Music*, *L'Allegro*, *Il Penseroso*, *Comus* and *Lycidas*, but even by the time he wrote *Lycidas*, when he was nearly thirty, Milton still felt unready for his great work, whatever it was to be.

In 1638 he visited Italy, the centre of European civilization (as well as the residence of the Pope) and spent about sixteen months there. He later wrote that Italy was 'the lodging place of *humanitas* and all the arts of civilization'. He read his Latin and Italian poems at literary societies, where they were much admired.

He returned to England in the summer of 1639. The country was riven by related political and religious controversies. Milton became involved in writing pamphlets against the episcopacy, urging that the work of the Reformation should be finished, and in defence of liberty 'religious, domestic and civil'. It seemed to be the dawning of a new glorious age, of which he hoped to be the poet, though, apart from a few sonnets, he was to write no poetry for nearly twenty years.

In 1643 he married Mary Powell, who was only sixteen. She left him about a month after their marriage, though she returned to him in 1645. Milton had obviously married totally unsuitably, and even before his wife left him he had begun to write *The Doctrine and Discipline of Divorce*, urging that incompatible partners should be allowed to divorce. In 1644 he wrote *Areopagitica*, in which he argued the value of the free publication of books and that truth would eventually triumph over error.

Charles I was executed in 1649 and shortly afterwards Milton wrote *The Tenure of Kings and Magistrates*, justifying regicide. He was employed by Cromwell to justify the execution of the King – in Latin, to a European audience. At this time Milton's eyesight began seriously to fail and by 1652 he was totally blind. Mary Powell died in 1655; he married Katherine Woodstock in 1656, but after a brief happy marriage she died in 1658.

Cromwell, whom Milton greatly admired, died in 1658, and the country fell under military rule. At the time of the Restoration in 1660 Milton was fifty-one years old, blind and disillusioned. His hopes had collapsed; and he was imprisoned for a short time – he must have considered himself lucky when he was set free. By that time he had already begun to write *Paradise Lost*.

Some difficulties of Milton's verse

Milton's verse has a range of reference which is outside the scope of most modern readers. He was a learned man, and he used his learning. Few of us can understand his verse without the help of notes, and even these must fail to convey the entire, spontaneously apprehended, range of reference which the poet intended. Short of becoming as learned as Milton, there is no way round this, but we should not be discouraged since he still has a great deal to offer. In any case it is doubtful whether Milton is as difficult to understand as, say, Donne or, because of his metaphorical complexity, Shakespeare.

In the last fifty years Milton's style has come under severe attack. Dr Johnson stated the matter succinctly in his *Life of Milton* when he said that Milton 'formed his style on a perverse and pedantic principle. He was desirous to use English words with a foreign idiom.' Dr F. R. Leavis has written, in *Revaluation*, of what he calls 'the monotony of the ritual' in *Paradise Lost*. 'Mere orotundity,' he says, 'is a disproportionate part of the effect.'

Milton does, undoubtedly, frequently twist the natural order of English words. Many of his sentences are long and their grammar is extraordinarily complex. The following passage, taken at random, comes from Book VIII and is found on page 91:

> Mine eyes he closed, but open left the cell
> Of fancy, my internal sight, by which
> Abstract as in a trance methought I saw,
> Though sleeping, where I lay, and saw the Shape
> Still glorious before whom awake I stood;
> Who stooping opened my left side, and took
> From thence a rib, with cordial spirits warm,
> And life-blood streaming fresh; wide was the wound,
> But suddenly with flesh filled up and healed.

Those who defend this style maintain that, by his manipulations of word order, Milton brings down the emphasis where he wants it and that, particularly when it is read aloud, the verse is not merely clear but also drops the ideas into the reader's mind with just the weight or contrast the poet intends. For instance, there is the contrast between 'closed' and 'open'; the emphasis on 'Abstract', which, holding back the rhythm momentarily, enacts the sense. Or the following short, maze-like phrases which reflect the dreamy nature of the experience; or the sudden gush of rhythm in 'And life-blood streaming fresh'. Undoubtedly, though, Milton does sometimes contort the English language. This is often particularly striking in passages of stilted dialogue, as when Eve says to the Serpent (p.95):

> How cam'st thou speakable of mute, and how
> To me so friendly grown above the rest
> Of brutal kind, that daily are in sight?
> Say, for such wonder claims attention due.

Readers can find an illuminating discussion of Milton's style, with copious illustrations of his successful local effects, in Christopher Ricks's *Milton's Grand Style*.

It ought to be added, however – obvious though it is – that Milton had no one single style; he believed there was a style that was appropriate, 'answerable', for the subject of a particular poem, and since in *Paradise Lost* he was writing of 'things unattempted yet in prose or rhyme' it is natural that the style should be magniloquent. Moreover, even in *Paradise Lost*, Milton was also master of great simplicities to which he repeatedly comes home. In fact, the poem may be said to be built on the skeleton of such simplicities. Here are just a few, chosen from Books I and II:

> I may assert Eternal Providence,
> And justify the ways of God to men . . .
> Who durst defy th' Omnipotent to arms . . .
> . . . What though the field be lost? . . .

... out of good still to find means of evil ...
Better to reign in Hell than serve in Heaven ...
My sentence is for open war ...
Which if not victory is yet revenge ...
      ... What if we find
Some easier enterprise? ...
        ... When his darling sons,
Hurled headlong to partake with us, shall curse
Their frail original, and faded bliss,
Faded so soon ...

Many, many examples of such command of direct, pithy English can be found throughout the poem.

The early poems

On The Morning of Christ's Nativity (page 21)

The poem was written in 1629, when Milton was twenty-one, and was intended as a birthday gift for Christ. It is a virtuoso piece, showing astonishing technical skill for one so young.

The ode is in two parts: first an Introduction, then the Hymn itself. The Introduction is grand, rotund, full of pomp; the 'Hymn' itself is composed of shorter, lighter lines, but both stanza-forms are rounded off with a winding Alexandrine.

The poem demands to be read – or rather 'declared' – aloud. In the Introduction each verse is a full musical period in itself, brought to a musical close. In verse IV Milton sees himself as anticipating the Wise Men by bringing a gift – the 'Hymn' – to the Christ-child.

The 'Hymn' is deliberately highly artificial. The Introduction is purely Christian in its references, but the 'Hymn' is full of classical allusions and ornate imagery. Milton is ready to lay all his hard-won learning at Christ's feet. He freely mixes the pagan with the Christian: sometimes he sees Christ as the fulfilment of what was only partial in the pagan world, so that Christ is referred to as 'the mighty Pan' – the true God of whom Pan was the shadow; elsewhere, Christ is seen as banishing the pagan deities back into the darkness from which they came.

Peace comes down 'with turtle wing'; all the paraphernalia of war is laid aside; the world of Nature is hushed; the stars wait upon 'the event'; the sun hides its head at the advent of the greater 'Sun'.

Before the revelation comes, however, we see 'the shepherds on the lawn', almost comically mundane, 'simply chatting in a rustic row'. They are concerned only with their own affairs, but upon them bursts the Music of the Spheres which will 'hold all Heav'n and Earth in happier union'. To hold heaven and earth in union is the very purpose of Incarnation.

Then the curtain goes up on the angelic choir singing music never heard since the Creation, 'when of old the sons of morning sang'. The spheres join in, serenading the earth in a divine concert, leading us back to the age of gold before the Fall. But the age of gold is not yet to be; 'wisest Fate' says no. The babe has still to be crucified, history to be lived through until the Last Judgment and the Second Coming: 'and then at last our bliss/Full and perfect is'. This, the Nativity, is the beginning of the New Age, limiting the 'usurped sway' of Satan, who is seen in Morality Play terms, and 'swinges the scaly horror of his folded tail'.

The coming of Christ banishes the pagan gods (who were thought to be the fallen angels). The Delphic oracle vanishes 'with hollow shriek'; the local pagan deities who were thought to people the countryside are more regretfully dismissed – 'nymphs in twilight shade of tangled thickets mourn'. The gods of the Israelites' enemies are more savagely treated, particularly 'sullen' Moloch, to whom human sacrifices were offered. The infant Christ destroys his pagan enemies, as Hercules, who had prefigured Christ, strangled snakes in his cradle.

In the penultimate stanza, Christ's coming is like the sunrise chasing away the ghosts of the pagan night. The last stanza focuses on the Virgin in the stable with her baby, with the 'youngest-teemed' star overhead; but the common stable is also a court attended by 'Bright-harnessed angels ... in order serviceable'.

The poem has been criticized as being too intellectual, too self-consciously elaborate, lacking intimacy and humanity, the humanity of the Incarnate Christ. Certainly it is a far cry from the almost monosyllabic simplicity of a medieval carol such as 'I sing of a maiden', and even further from Christmas-card-like holly, snow and mistletoe. It is lofty and imposing and, characteristically of Milton, places Christ as the central event in the vastness of cosmic history.

holy sages The Old Testament prophets
our deadly forfeit Death, the penalty of the Fall
insufferable Too bright to look at
Trinal Unity Father, Son and Holy Spirit
a darksome house of mortal clay The human body, with its
   limitations, inhabited by the spirit
vein The gift of poetry
afford Offer
the sun's team The horses of the sun-god's chariot, drawing the
   sun across the sky
spangled host Stars
the star-led wizards The Wise Men
prevent Go before

had doffed her gaudy trim Had put off the rich 'clothes' of
   summer
paramour Lover; the source of the earth's fertility
guilty front Front = forehead. Nature is 'guilty' because it fell
   at the same time as Man.
Confounded Ashamed
to cease To end
the turning sphere The shell of the heavens surrounding the
   earth
turtle Dove's; the dove is a symbol of peace
She strikes a universal peace through sea and land At the
   time of Christ's birth the Pax Romana was said to have prevailed
   in the Roman Empire.

hooked Chariots had scythe-like blades attached to their wheels
awful Full of awe
whist Hushed
rave Go wild
birds of calm The halcyon, a fabulous bird, rested on the sea's
   surface during December.

influence Astrological term for the power of the heavenly bodies

For all Despite all

Lucifer The 'Son of the Morning', who fell from Heaven, through pride

Orbs Heavenly spheres

a greater Sun Christ

burning axletree The axle of the sun's chariot

page 24

lawn Field

the mighty Pan The shepherds' god. Christ, the good shepherd, was referred to as 'the true Pan'.

kindly Lovingly; also, 'according to his kind', or according to Nature

took Captivated

close A cadence in music

the hollow round/Of Cynthia's seat The sphere of the moon

won Persuaded

To think her part was done To think that the end of the world had come

unexpressive Inexpressible

page 25

when of old the sons of morning sung At the creation 'when the morning stars sang together and all the sons of God shouted for joy' (Job 38,7)

welt'ring Heaving

Ring out, ye crystal spheres According to the Pythagorean–Platonic idea, the spheres, each producing a separate note, made a sublime, nine-part harmony, inaudible to human ears

consort Accompaniment

the age of gold The classical Golden Age was a period of innocence and happiness which Christians often identified with life in Eden before the Fall

speckled Vanity The stain of human sin

mould Substance

Justice There is an allusion to Astraea, the star-maiden of Greek legend, who left earth at the time of the Golden Age and whose return will herald a new Golden Age.

sheen Radiance

tissued Interwoven with golden and silver light

page 26

those ychained in sleep Those imprisoned by death

wakeful Arousing

With such a horrid clang In this passage the thunder and lightning which accompanied the presentation to Moses of the Ten Commandments is compared to the Last Judgment. The word 'horrid' had an authentically strong meaning in Milton's day. It is derived from the Latin 'horrere', to bristle. Something horrid makes the hair stand on end.

session The word was pronounced with three syllables.

Dragon Satan

straiter Narrower

his usurped sway His power which he has illegally seized

the steep of Delphos Apollo's oracle was at Delphi, on a Greek mountainside. In this and the following stanza the pagan Greek world has passed away, superseded by the Christian.

page 27

Genius Presiding spirit

Lars and Lemures Local gods and spirits of ancient Rome

flamens Priests

quaint Elaborate

peculiar Belonging to a particular place

Peor Baal, the god of the Phoenicians

Baalim Pronounced with three syllables. Baal's lesser gods.

that twice-battered god of Palestine Dagon, the god of the Philistines, whose image was broken twice

Ashtaroth A moon goddess

girt Surrounded

Libyc Hammon shrinks his horn An Egyptian God with a ram's head, worshipped in Libya

the Tyrian maids their wounded Thammuz mourn
  Tyrian = Phoenician. Thammuz was the Phoenician name for
  Adonis, a vegetation deity.
Moloch The pagan sun-god. Human sacrifices were offered to
  him.
brutish Egyptian gods, such as Isis, Orus and Anubis, had animal
  heads.

page 28

Osiris Chief of the Egyptian gods, represented as a bull, with a
  shrine at Memphis
his sacred chest The image of Osiris was carried in a small
  tabernacle ('chest') accompanied by tambourine music.
sable-stoled Dressed in black
eyn Eyes
Typhon The evil, Egyptian, serpentine god
Can in his swaddling bands control the damned crew Christ
  is compared to Hercules who, while he was still in his cradle,
  strangled two snakes
orient Eastern
shadows Ghosts, which had to return to the underworld at dawn
several Separate
fays Fairies
maze Place for dancing
youngest-teemed star Most recently born – the star that guided
  the Wise Men
car Chariot
bright-harnessed Dressed in bright armour
serviceable Ready to serve

On Shakespeare (page 29)

The poem appeared in the Second Folio of Shakespeare's
plays, published in 1632. It is an epitaph, and combines a
necessary formality with affection. He is '*my* Shakespeare' and
'*Dear* son of memory'. There is reference to the belief that
Shakespeare wrote easily and naturally: we are told in the

Preface to the First Folio (1632) that he 'never blotted a line', and Milton refers in *L'Allegro* to Shakespeare warbling 'his native woodnotes wild'.

Through the poem runs an ingenious 'conceit' (an expanded metaphor) that Shakespeare needs no monument, no 'star-ypointing pyramid': he has made us, his readers, 'a livelong monument' by taking our imaginations away from us, leaving us like marble or, as it were, turned to stone.

What For what.
relics Remains
son of Memory The Muses were the daughters of Memory: Shakespeare is therefore referred to as their brother
numbers Verses
unvalued Invaluable
Delphic Apollo's oracle was at Delphi. Milton is referring to the prophetic power of poetry.
fancy Imagination
bereaving Robbing
conceiving Imagining

On the University Carrier (page 30)

Thomas Hobson drove a weekly coach between Cambridge and London, and must have been a familiar figure to Cambridge undergraduates. He died in 1631, aged eighty-seven.

This is a light, playful and affectionate piece. The images are all taken from Hobson's occupation as a carrier. Mr Weller, another carrier, uses the same device in his famous letter about his wife's death in *Pickwick Papers*. The language is colloquial – ''Twas such a shifter'. And the images – for example, that Hobson was so constantly on the move that Death had difficulty in tracking him down – are good-humoured and homely.

vacancy Period of idleness
girt Girth

slough Mud hole
'Twas such a shifter He was so constantly on the move
The Bull Hobson's coaching station in London
latest Last
chamberlain The chief servant of an inn

L'Allegro and Il Penseroso (pages 31–4)

The two poems are a matching pair and are best treated together. They were probably written during a vacation from Cambridge. In their full version both poems are three times as long as the extracts given here.

'L'Allegro' means 'the cheerful, happy, sanguine man'; 'Il Penseroso' means 'the contemplative, melancholy man'. They describe idealized, complementary worlds. *L'Allegro* is associated with youth and sociability; *Il Penseroso* is associated with maturity and solitude.

In *L'Allegro* the world and its innocent pleasures are celebrated; 'sweet Liberty' is something to be enjoyed, because the world is unfallen, so welcome Jest, Innocent Flirtation, Sport, Laughter, Dancing, Liberty, Mirth, Hymen, Stage-comedy, Music.

The full poem describes a day in the life of the contented man: the two extracts which we are given describe dawn and night. The metre is light-footed octosyllabics.

In *Il Penseroso* the octosyllabics are sobered and slowed: Peace, Fast, Contemplation, Silence, Study are invoked: through these things 'old experience' may, in the end, 'atain/ To something like prophetic strain'; the introspective man may learn to 'see into the life of things'.

Dr Johnson, in his *Life of Milton*, wrote, 'The author's design is not ... merely to show how objects derive their colours from the mind, by representing the operation of the same things upon the gay and melancholy temper, or upon the same man as he is differently disposed; but rather how, among the successive variety of appearances, every disposition of mind takes hold on those by which it may be gratified.' So, the first addresses a Nymph, the second a Nun; the first hears the lark, the second the nightingale; the first goes to the theatre, the second walks 'the studious cloister'; the first hears 'soft Lydian airs', the second 'anthems clear'; and so on.

It is worth mentioning, since Milton is often caricatured as a stern unbending old Puritan, that he had more than one side to his nature. *L'Allegro* is not to be superseded by *Il Penseroso*: they are to be held in equal balance. *L'Allegro* is particuarly moving when it celebrates the sensuous charms of music:

> Such strains as would have won the ear
> Of Pluto, to have quite set free
> His half-regained Eurydice.

The cadence is ravishing as the music itself.

page 31

Nymph Euphrosyne, or Mirth, one of the three Graces, the daughter either of Venus, goddess of love, and Bacchus, god of wine and revelry, or of Zephyr, the west wind, and Aurora, the dawn

Cranks Jokes, witty speech

Becks Nods of welcome

Hebe Jove's daughter, the cup-bearer of the gods

fantastic Agile, as in a dance

Hymen The god of marriage

saffron robe, with taper clear The traditional attributes of Hymen

masque Hymen was often a character in masques of the period. A masque was a dramatic spectacular, with music and dancing, in which actors personified mythological deities, shepherdesses, etc.

antique Old-fashioned, or in imitation of the ancients

Jonson's learned sock A sock was a low-heeled, light shoe,
worn by actors in Greek comedy. Ben Jonson wrote learned,
neo-Classical comedies.

Fancy's child Milton regarded Shakespeare, by contrast with
Jonson, as an instinctive writer of comedies in the native tradition.

against In order to prevent

Lydian airs The Lydian mode, one of the Greek 'modes' of
music, each of which produced a particular emotional effect, was
soft and relaxing.

meeting The soul, freed from the body, goes to 'meet' the music.
These lines describe the effect of the Lydian mode.

Orpheus The most famous poet of Greek legend

Of Pluto, to have quite set free/His half-regained Eurydice
Orpheus's eloquent song persuaded Pluto, the ruler of Hell, to
release his dead wife Eurydice: but Orpheus looked back as he
led her out of Hell, which was against his agreement with
Pluto, so Eurydice, 'half-regained', was lost again. The lines
charmingly fancy that these Lydian airs would have freed
Eurydice completely.

grain Colour

sable stole of cypress lawn robe of fine black material

state Behaviour

commercing Communicating

Forget thyself to marble When the soul is 'rapt' it forgets
the body, which becomes like a marble statue, without a
soul. (See *On Shakespeare*, line 14.)

sad Serious

diet Dine. Abstinence is associated with mystical vision.

Guiding the fiery-wheeled throne The cherubs, one of the
angelic orders, drew God's chariot-throne. (See Ezekiel, 1,10.)

Contemplation The cherubs contemplated the divine mysteries

hist Draws

Philomel The nightingale

page 34

Cynthia The moon-goddess, whose chariot was drawn by dragons
pale Enclosure
embowed Arched
With antic pillars massy proof The massive, richly decorated
 pillars of an old church
storied With stories in stained glass
dight Decorated
spell Study
prophetic strain The gift of prophecy is acquired through living
 a spare, ascetic life.

How soon hath Time (page 35)

This sonnet was probably written in 1632, when Milton was
living with his parents and continuing his prolonged self-
education by following a rigorous course of reading. He may
have been reminded by his father, or by friends, that he was
twenty-three and had still achieved nothing; in any case, he
would have been acutely conscious of this himself. He replies
that he is taking his time, preparing himself, and the 'will of
Heav'n' is leading him on. The poem is self-confident without arrogance, mature despite the professed lack of 'inward
ripeness'. It shows the earnestness with which he regarded
poetry as a calling.

 The sonnet is conventional in form: the first eight lines are
divided into two halves, but the main change of gear occurs
smoothly at the 'Yet' at the beginning of the sestet. The last
two lines sum up.

career Speedy course
semblance Outward appearance. Milton is supposed to have
 looked younger than he was.
endu'th Is bestowed upon
strictest measure ev'n At a steady pace
**All is, if I have grace to use it so, / As ever in my great
 Task-Master's eye** All that matters is, whether I have grace
 to use Time in the knowledge that God is always watching.

At a Solemn Music (page 30)

The 'argument' of the poem is, briefly, as follows: Voice and Verse together are 'pledges of heav'n's joy', intimations of the divine life while we are still on earth. They breathe life into the dead and are an echo of the music which the Seraphim, the Cherubim and the Saints are 'singing everlastingly'. Once, Nature and 'all creatures' sang and played such music, but 'disproportioned sin / Jarred against Nature's chime'. (In the same way we cannot hear the Music of the Spheres because 'this muddy vesture of decay / Doth grossly close it in' – *The Merchant of Venice*, Act V, Scene i, 64–5.) The poem ends with the prayer that we may soon be joined with that 'celestial consort'.

In *Lycidas*, Milton says that Edward King 'knew / Himself to sing and build the lofty rhyme', and the quotation is an apt description of this poem. First, the poem has a *singing* quality. We must not be misled by the word 'solemn' in the title, which today has heavily funereal overtones: to Milton it meant 'ceremonious and celebratory', so that 'solemn jubilee' is no paradox. The poem is not a dirge, but a shout of joy, a 'melodious noise'. Secondly, the poem is 'built' architecturally, phrase upon clause upon phrase. The first sentence (there are only two) is twenty-four lines long, yet Milton is always in control as it modulates through lines of varying length and irregular rhyme to its close. Thirdly, the poem is undoubtedly 'lofty', but neither overblown nor pompous. Milton is often praised, sometimes disparaged, for his 'organ music'; but an organ has many stops and many colours; it can be a bright as well as a resounding instrument.

Sirens The spirits governing the spheres of the heavens, each singing a different note and together making the 'music of the spheres'. Here, 'Voice and Verse'.

Dead things with inbreathed sense able to pierce Able to breathe life into dead things, as Orpheus charmed rocks and trees

phantasy Imagination
consent Harmony
jubilee Exultant joy
just spirits Souls of the blessed dead
Nature's chime The harmony that prevailed before the Fall
diapason Harmony covering the complete range of notes
consort A symphony, or an orchestra of musicians employed by
  a great household

from **Comus** (pages 37–42)

Comus is a masque which was presented at Ludlow Castle in
1634. It was performed by the three children and friends of
the Earl of Bridgewater on his inauguration as Lord President
of Wales. It had music by Henry Lawes, one of the most dis-
tinguished composers of his time. Dancing and spectacle were
always central ingredients of the masque. The complete work
is just over a thousand lines long.

Comus shows the triumph of virtue over vice and propounds
'the sage and serious doctrine of Virginity'. The situation is
that the Lady and her two brothers are going home through
a 'drear wood', but the Lady has become separated from her
brothers. Comus – son of Bacchus, god of wine, and Circe, the
enchantress who turned men into animals – lies in wait to
seduce them, to mislead them into his 'sensual sty'. The stage
direction says: 'Comus enters, with a charming-rod in his
hand, his glass in the other; with him a rout of monsters,
headed like sundry sorts of wild beasts, but otherwise like men
and women, their apparel glistering; they come in making a
riotous and unruly noise, with torches in their hands.' Comus,
therefore, is a deceiver, superficially attractive, representing
the animal part of man, bringing disorder and dis-harmony.

His speech begins apparently innocently and attractively –
evil is powerless unless it is attractive – in light tripping
rhythms reminiscent of *L'Allegro*; but the dance is 'tipsy';
Rigour, Advice, Age and Severity are mocked and dismissed.
''Tis only daylight that makes sin' expresses the amorality of

'anything goes'. Nature itself – the 'Sounds, and Seas, with all their finny drove' – is dancing; fairies, elves and wood-nymphs 'their merry wakes and pastimes keep', and it is by an appeal to the wantonness of Nature that Comus is to tempt the Lady.

Soon, however, the speech moves from the comparatively innocent to the mention of Cotytto, whose pagan rites were celebrated in sexual orgies, and of Hecate the witch. The atmosphere becomes thick with evil as 'Stygian darkness spets her thickest gloom'. This is what has become of 'the better sweets of night'. The rhythms become more frenzied, culminating in 'The Measure': a wild dance, described in the stage-direction to the Cambridge manuscript as 'a wild, rude and wanton antic'.

As the Lady approaches, Comus announces his intentions like a melodramatic villain. A virgin 'benighted in these woods' is perfect prey. He turns to his 'charms' and 'dazzling spells'. In rather the same way Satan, in *Paradise Lost*, waylays Eve with 'false presentments'.

Comus's speech beginning 'O foolishness of men' comes from much later in the masque and is the central temptation. It is a brilliant dramatic performance and uses his knowledge of rhetoric and his poetic skills to give the tempter a wonderful run for his money. Dr F. R. Leavis, in his largely derogatory essay on Milton's verse in *Revaluation*, claims that the speech is 'richer, subtler and more sensitive than anything in *Paradise Lost*, *Paradise Regained* or *Samson Agonistes*'.

The speech is, indeed, sensuously very rich. Note the grating contempt of '*budge* doctors' and 'fetch their precepts from the cynic tub'; the scarecrow thinness of 'lean and sallow Abstinence'; the accumulated emphasis on 'pour' – one of those useful English words which has an uncertain number of syllables and which is positioned in the line so as to go on and on; the thickly crowding consonants in 'Thronging the seas with spawn innumerable'; the epicurean superiority implied in 'the *curious* taste'; what Dr Leavis calls 'the impression of the swarming worms telescoped with that of the ordered industry of the workshop'; the heavy sag in the middle of the line on '*surcharged*'; the six heavy stresses in 'Th' earth cumbered and the winged air darkened with plumes', where the words are like blocks to shut out the light; the solidity of '*bestud* with stars' which seems to make the stars three-dimensional.

The argument is that the overflowing bounty of Nature is there to be used and enjoyed. Comus then moves on to urge that the Lady's beauty

> is nature's coin, must not be hoarded,
> But must be current; and the good thereof
> Consists in mutual and partaken bliss.

He adds flattery of her 'Love-darting eyes and tresses like the morn' and reminds her that beauty is transient and

> If you let slip time, like a neglected rose
> It withers on the stalk with languished head.

So 'gather ye rose-buds'.

Comus's case is powerful, vividly expressed and not easy to answer, and the Lady's speech inevitably lacks the vivid particularity of Comus's. In fact she suffers no temptation, which is no doubt to the detriment of the piece as *drama*; but the masque is not a drama in the sense we have come to expect from, for instance, a Shakespeare play. She speaks with lofty scorn – 'I had not thought to have unlocked my lips' – which is in some danger of sounding merely prim; but she *knows*, with complete intuition, that Comus is a juggler. She does not entirely refuse, however, to answer his arguments: she replies to his appeal to the fertility of Nature by pointing out that only a pampered few can enjoy luxury while many a 'just man now pines with want', and that it would be better if 'Nature's full blessings' were 'well dispensed / In unsuperfluous ev'n proportion'. This recalls Gloucester in *King Lear*: 'distribution should undo excess / And each man have enough'.

The second part of the Lady's reply also recalls *King Lear*, where Albany says, 'Wisdom and goodness to the vile seem vile; filths savour but themselves.' The Lady disdains to expound 'the sage / And serious doctrine of Virginity' on the grounds that Comus has 'nor ear nor soul to apprehend' it. This is no doubt true, though the reader may feel deprived. No doubt the doctrine is also too much of a 'sublime notion and high mystery' to be uttered. She leaves him to enjoy his own world of 'dear wit and gay rhetoric', merely asserting that if she *were* to put her case, 'all thy magic structures' would be 'shattered in heaps o'er thy false head'.

The extract ends, much more abruptly than the full original, with a 'moral' which, in the circumstances, can hardly avoid sounding rather neatly trite.

Page 37

fold Put his sheep in the fold

car of Day The sun's chariot, which has sunk into the Atlantic, in the west

slope Descended

rosy twine A wreath of roses

Advice Consideration

saws Wise moral sayings

We that are of purer fire Comus and his spirits, Comus claims, are made of fire, the highest of the four elements.

the starry quire The music of the spheres

watchful The stars are watchful because they belong to the sphere of fire which guards the unchanging upper world against the changing lower world, the earth.

sounds Bodies of water

morris A dance

Page 38

wakes Nocturnal festivities

'Tis only daylight that makes sin 'Out of sight, out of mind'

dun Dark

Cotytto A Thracian goddess whose rites were celebrated at night and accompanied by wild orgies

the dragon womb / Of Stygian darkness spets her thickest gloom Night is seen as the product of a dragon spitting darkness from its belly ('womb'). The association of darkness with evil was deep-rooted.

ebon Ebony, black

Hecat' Hecate, originally a moon-goddess, but later identified with Persephone; in the end she was regarded as the mistress of midnight devils and spectres and a teacher of sorcery. Comus's captives are forced to worship her.

the blabbing eastern scout The morning, which spies on and reports their festivity to the tell-tale sun

nice Prudish

round Dance

The Measure The dance of the evil characters which is broken off when Comus hears the Lady's approach

shrouds Hiding-places

brakes Thickets

trains Snares

my mother Circe Circe changed men into beasts by a magic potion, a power which Comus inherits

spongy Absorbent

page 39

blear Dim, indistinct in outline

false presentments Hallucinations

quaint habits Strange dress

budge doctors of the Stoic fur, / And fetch their precepts from the Cynic tub The hoods of learned men were made of lambskin fur ('budge'). The word is used contemptuously. The Stoic and Cynic philosophers of Greece advocated plain living. Diogenes, the famous Cynic, lived in a tub.

sate Satisfy or glut

curious Fastidious

green shops The silk worms' 'shops' are the green leaves on which they feed.

hutched Enclosed
th' all-worshipped ore Gold
store Provide
pet A momentary peevish impulse
pulse Beans and peas
frieze Coarse woollen cloth. Milton seems to have missed the
  pun on 'freeze'!
who i.e. Nature
surcharged Over-burdened
waste Superfluous
cumbered Obstructed (by excess)
darked with plumes Darkened by birds' wings
over-multitude their lords Multiply beyond the control of man

page 40

The sea o'erfraught would swell The sea would be so
  over-populated with fish that it would swell
th' unsought diamonds ... shameless brows The diamonds
  that nobody was bothering to look for would create such a
  glare in the sea that the gods and creatures at the bottom of
  the sea would grow used to the light and leave their naturally
  dark element to look shamelessly at the sun. A pleasing fantasy!
coy Falsely modest
cozened Deceived
partaken Shared
brag Occasion for boasting
homely features Plain-faced girls – i.e. not the Lady
sorry grain Coarse texture
will serve to play / The sampler Will be good enough to work
  at the embroidery – with which the Lady need not bother her
  pretty head!
tease Comb out
vermeil-tinctured Red
juggler Deceiving magician; clever talker
pranked Flashily dressed up
bolt sift, refine
Means her provision only to the good Intends her gifts only
  for good people

page 41

beseeming Suitable
dispensed Shared out
no whit encumbered Not at all overburdened
Crams, and blasphemes his Feeder Gorges himself, which is
 a blasphemy against God the giver
Enjoy your dear wit Enjoy the cleverness you're so proud of
fence The power of playing with words or chopping logic
convinced Refuted
uncontrolled Unlimited
pure cause The doctrine of virginity
moved to sympathize Moved in sympathy
lend her nerves Contribute her strength

page 42

the sphery chime The music of the spheres

from **Lycidas** (page 43)

The occasion for the writing of this poem was the death by
drowning in the Irish Sea of Edward King. He died in 1637
at the age of twenty-five. Milton was an acquaintance of his
at Cambridge – not, apparently, a close friend. King was a
learned young man who was dedicated to a career in the
Church. The poem first appeared in a memorial volume to
King, contributed by various hands, in which there were
twenty-three poems in Latin and Greek and thirteen in
English.

The poem belongs to a long tradition of the pastoral elegy,
a very ancient and sophisticated art-form in which shepherds
and pastoral life are used as a disguise for talking about something else – in this case, young poets. The mode may seem
unreal to the modern reader, as, indeed, it was to Dr Johnson,
who wrote in his *Life of Milton*: 'its inherent improbability
always forces dissatisfaction on the mind'. He quotes the lines

beginning 'We drove afield' and comments: 'We know that they never drove afield, and that they had no flocks to batten; and though it be allowed that the representation may be allegorical, the true meaning is so uncertain and remote that it is never sought, because it cannot be known when it is found.'

Clearly we must, in Coleridge's famous phrase, 'suspend our disbelief' and accept the conventions of pastoral poetry if the poem is to be understood and enjoyed; then we may find that the pastoral convention universalizes the sense of loss even while it distances it. Johnson complained that 'where there is leisure for fiction there is little grief', but the poem is not intended to be a passionate and spontaneous outburst of grief for a particular dead friend. Edward King is the type of the promising young poet/priest cut off before his prime.

An astonishing judgment which Johnson makes is that 'the diction is harsh', 'the rhymes uncertain, the numbers unpleasing'. This seems a reflection on 18th-century taste rather than on Milton. There can hardly be a more mellifluous poem in the language.

In the first section, Milton is picking laurels for the dead poet prematurely, while the berries are still 'harsh and crude'. The sense of violent outrage in Lycidas's early death is expressed in the brutal '*Shatter* your leaves before the mellowing year'. Milton's sense of his own unreadiness is in the reference to his 'forced fingers rude': he has not yet finished preparing himself.

The second section asks *why* King should have died so young. The question is universalized by the reference to Orpheus, torn violently to pieces and thrown into the Hebrus. What is the good of the strenuous life of study, self-discipline, of scorning delights and living laborious days, if the 'thin-spun' life is to be so prematurely 'slit'? Would it not be better to accept Comus's advice and 'sport with Amaryllis in the shade'? But he recalls to himself that Fame, which is 'the spur', is also 'no plant that grows on mortal soil': the only 'perfect witness' is 'all-judging Jove'.

There follows the famous attack on the supine Church of England. The pastoral convention was frequently used to attack things that it might be dangerous to attack more directly, and lends itself well to such a subject since 'pastors' are shepherds. A line such as 'the hungry sheep look up and are not fed' is wholly appropriate in context. The passage is a superb effusion of controlled Miltonic spleen, full of vigorously contemptuous verbs – 'Creep and intrude and climb', 'scramble', 'shove away': and the onomatopoeia of 'their lean and flashy songs / Grate on their scrannel pipes of wretched straw' is ear-piercing. (It is sad that 'scrannel' is lost to the language.) Whether the passage can be justified as part of the 'argument' of the poem is more doubtful; but it may be argued that the clergy represent the evil and slothful who are allowed to survive while such men as Edward King die.

The last section celebrates the resurrection, in the light of which all human sorrows should be viewed. Lycidas is 'not dead', but 'mounted high / Through the dear might of Him who walked the waves' – the image of 'walking the waves' is in answer to King's drowning. The poem comes to a quiet end as the evening falls and the shepherd looks to 'fresh woods and pastures new' in the morning. The last line suggests the living world: Milton is perhaps bidding farewell to the pastoral convention; or looking forward to his Italian journey; or planning larger poetic tasks.

The poem is one of those – like, for instance, Gray's *Elegy* – from which people quote frequently without having read a word of the poem, and without realizing they are quoting from it. This suggests that, despite the artificiality of its conventions, or perhaps *because* of them, the poem speaks with memorable finality about the common human lot.

page 43

Lycidas A pastoral name
Yet once more Milton had abandoned his plan not to write

again until he was ready to write his great epic; Edward King
deserved an elegy

laurels Laurels, myrtles and ivy are evergreen plants from which
poets' garlands were made

crude Unripe

dear Of intimate concern to the writer

welter Be tossed

meed Reward

Sisters of the sacred well The Muses; the sacred well is the
Pierian Spring under Mount Olympus

destined urn The tomb I am destined for

high lawns Smooth hillsides

What time the grey-fly winds her sultry horn The hum of
the insects in the noonday heat

page 44

batt'ning Feeding

**Where were ye, Nymphs ... Nor yet where Deva spreads
her wizard stream** Where were the nymphs, who love poets,
when Lycidas was drowned? The 'steep' is perhaps
Penmaenmawr, opposite Anglesey; Mona is Anglesey; Deva is the
the river Dee, which is 'wizard' because it can, allegedly,
miraculously change its course. These places are all near where
Edward King was drowned.

fondly Foolishly

**What could the Muse herself ... Down the swift Hebrus
to the Lesbian shore?** The Muse is Calliope, mother of
Orpheus the great mythical poet, who enchanted Nature with his
song but was torn to pieces by a crowd ('rout') of Thracian
women. His head was thrown into the River Hebrus and floated
to the isle of Lesbos. If the Muse could not save her own son,
what chance had Edward King?

boots Profits

homely slighted shepherd's trade The undervalued art of
poetry

meditate Study

use Are accustomed to do

Amaryllis ... Neaera Shepherd girls

clear Noble
guerdon Reward
the blind Fury Atropos, one of the Fates. Milton calls her a
  Fury, and 'blind', like Fortune, to emphasize her irrationality.
Phoebus Apollo, the sun-god, and the god of poetry
foil The setting of a jewel

page 45

Camus The god of the river Cam, at Cambridge
sedge Grass. Camus is dressed plainly, as befits the scholarly.
that sanguine flower The hyacinth. Hyacinth, in legend, was a
  Spartan boy who was loved by Apollo, who accidentally killed
  him. The flower sprang from the boy's blood ('sanguine').
inscribed with woe On the hyacinth were marks which looked
  like the Greek for 'alas!'.
reft Snatched away
pledge Child. King had been a student and Fellow of Christ's
  College, Cambridge.
The Pilot of the Galilean lake St Peter
Two massy keys The keys of Heaven (see Matthew 16,19)
amain With force
mitred locks St Peter was the first bishop
Of other care they little reck'ning make They care little for
  their pastoral duties
Blind mouths The priests are blind when they should see, and
  eat when they should feed others
What recks it them? What does it matter to them?
They are sped They are all right, looked after
lean and flashy songs Thin and ostentatious sermons. (Contrast
  Lycidas's 'lofty rhyme'.)
scrannel Thin and squeaky
draw Breathe in
wolf The greedy church, probably the Roman church in
  particular
privy Secret
**But that two-handed engine at the door / Stands ready to
  smite once and smite no more** Nobody is sure what these
  lines mean, though they have an apocalyptic ring. Perhaps the

'engine' is the sword of Michael, which will smite off Satan's head: or perhaps the lines refer to the two Houses of Parliament, ready to strike down the Roman church, 'the grim wolf with privy paw'. There are said to be twenty-eight separate explanations of the lines.

page 46

the day-star The sun
tricks Adorns
ore Gold
him that walked the waves Christ, whose walking on the waves was a parallel to Lycidas's resurrection after drowning
oozy Wet
laves Washes
unexpressive Inexpressible. The song represents the redeemed soul's mystical marriage with God.
And wipe the tears for ever from his eyes Revelation 7,17: 'And God shall wipe away all tears from their eyes.'
flood Sea
uncouth Unknown
quills Reeds
Doric lay Pastoral song
the sun had stretched out all the hills i.e. as the shadows lengthen in the evening
twitched Put on
blue Traditional for shepherds' cloaks

When I consider (page 47)

By 1652 Milton was totally blind. It seemed that 'that one Talent which is death to hide' was 'lodg'd with me useless'. The first seven and a half lines, winding insistently, exactly dramatize the mood of complaint, tinged with self-pity. *Paradise Lost* was written to 'justify the ways of God to man', but here Milton has a job to justify them to himself. In the eighth line, however, he recognizes that the questions are foolish and his discontent comes up against the rock of Patience. Patience is a Christian virtue and had a much stronger meaning in the 17th century (and in Shakespeare) than it has today, when it tends to mean little more than the ability to wait for a bus without losing your temper. It meant, then, the ability to bear real affliction without despair. Patience speaks gently, soothingly, modestly – compare the voice of Love in George Herbert's *Love Bade Me Welcome* – and reminds the poet of his small place in the scheme of things: 'God doth not need / Either man's work or his own gifts', and in the last line the poet puts himself firmly in his proper place. One may suspect, however, that 'standing and waiting' were not Milton's strong point; but then neither did his talent prove, in fact, useless.

talent See the parable of the talents in St Matthew. A talent was a piece of money, but here represents the poet's gift.
fondly Foolishly
thousands Of angels
They also serve who only stand and wait As well as the reference to Milton's own condition, there is perhaps a reference also to the highest order of angels, whose office is contemplation.

Cyriack, this three years' day (pages 47–8)

The poem was written in 1655. Cyriack Skinner was a young friend of Milton's.

  This poem, too, deals with the problems of his blindness, but more proudly and assertively. He will not bate 'a jot / Of heart or hope'; he is proud to have lost his sight 'In liberty's defence'. His defence of Cromwell's government is, he claims, the talk of Europe. (John Aubrey supports this by saying that 'he was much more admired abroad than at home'.)

this three years' day It is three years to the day since Milton went blind
though clear / To outward view Milton said that his eyes, though blind, appeared to be unclouded and bright
bate a jot Lose the tiniest bit

conscience The awareness of having lost his sight in the defence of liberty. He was Cromwell's Latin Secretary.

Of which all Europe talks Milton wrote his *Defence of the English People* in Latin for a European audience

masque Masquerade

had I no better guide i.e. than his faith in God

On his Deceased Wife (page 48)

Milton's second marriage, to Katherine Woodstock, seems to have been happy, but it was short-lived. He married her in November 1656 and she died, together with their baby daughter, in February 1658. The tone of the sonnet is restrained as he describes how he had dreamed that he had seen his dead wife: 'Her face was veiled, yet to my fancied sight / Love, sweetness, goodness in her person shined'. But, as often happens in dreams, he wakes up at the vital moment, as she leans over to embrace him. 'I wak'd, she fled, and day brought back my night' is a potent expression of his sense of loss. Day, to him, is night, since he is blind: the night is also the long night of his deprivation.

saint The usual term for a dead person

Alcestis The wife of King Admetus, who chose to die instead of her husband, and was restored to him from the underworld by Jove's son Hercules – showing some similarities to Christ

Mine, as whom washed from spot of child-bed taint The Mosaic law prescribed the purification of women after childbirth.

Full sight Milton had probably never seen his wife's face. According to St Paul we shall see 'face to face' in heaven.

Questions on the early poems

1 How does Milton combine the pagan and the Christian in *The Nativity Ode*?

2 Does *The Nativity Ode* manage to unify its disparate elements?

3 Discuss Warton's comment on *the Nativity Ode*: 'The *Ode* chiefly consists of a string of affected conceits, which his early youth, and the fashion of the times, can only excuse.'

4 Illustrate Milton's use of the 'conceit'.

5 Illustrate, from the early poems, the lighter and more playful side of Milton's mind.

6 How does Milton use the idea of music, and imagery from music, in the early poems?

7 Dr Johnson wrote of Milton's *Sonnets*: 'They deserve not any particular criticism; for the best it can only be said, that they are not bad.' Is this fair? Illustrate your answer by close reference to *two* sonnets.

8 Illustrate the force with which Comus tempts the Lady in *Comus*.

9 How would you answer the charge that Comus wins the argument with the Lady, and that the Lady only escapes by refusing to answer him?

10 What qualities does Comus share with Satan?

11 What is the real theme of *Lycidas*?

12 Discuss Dr Johnson's comment on *Lycidas*: 'It is not to be considered as the effusion of real passion; for passion runs not after remote allusions and obscure opinions.'

13 What is the function of the 'pastoral convention' in *Lycidas*?

14 If Milton had died before the Civil war would he be regarded merely as a minor poet?

The later poems

Paradise Lost

Ever since he was a boy Milton had been determined to write a great poem – great in subject-matter as well as in execution – which would rival, in his native tongue, the great epics of Latin, Greek and Italian. He felt that he was being led on to this by 'the will of Heaven' and with extraordinary steadiness of nerve and confidence in his destiny he devoted himself to study over many years until the time of 'inward ripeness' had arrived. (See Sonnet VII, p.35.)

For a long time Milton was uncertain as to the subject-matter of his poem, even of the form it would take. In 1639 he was still thinking of writing about King Arthur; at one time he listed a hundred possible subjects, some from British history, some from the Bible. By 1640 he seems to have decided that his great work would be a dramatic tragedy on the Greek model, and he made more than one draft of such a work on the subject, now, of Paradise lost, perhaps to be called 'Adam unparadiz'd'. Some lines of this tragedy were written and later incorporated into *Paradise Lost*.

All these plans were abandoned while Milton involved himself in the politics of the time. The poem as we know it seems to have been begun in 1658 and finished in 1663. It was printed in 1667. Milton was given an immediate payment of £5. The poem brought him a large measure of recognition, both from the more discerning of his countrymen and from foreigners who came to visit him.

It may be helpful to give a very brief summary of each of the twelve books of the poem.

Book I Satan and his followers are in Hell, following their expulsion from Heaven. Satan addresses his troops, reviving them. They may, he says, regain Heaven or some new world. Pandemonium is built as a council-chamber.

Book II The senior devils debate their future. Beelzebub proposes that they ruin God's new creation. Satan volunteers to undertake the task alone. He meets Sin and Death at the gates of Hell and voyages through Chaos.

Book III Heaven. God sees Satan coming and knows that he will succeed. The Son offers himself as Man's Redeemer. Meanwhile, Satan finds his way to Earth.

Book IV Satan Comes to Eden, sees Adam and Eve, and overhears them discussing the Tree of Knowledge. He tries to tempt Eve in a dream, but is discovered by Gabriel, who has come to defend Man. Satan flies.

Book V Adam and Eve at worship and work. Raphael warns them of their danger and describes Satan's rebellion in Heaven.

Book VI Raphael describes the three days' war in Heaven and repeats his warning to Adam.

Book VII Raphael describes to Adam and Eve the creation of the world.

Book VIII Adam tells Raphael how he is forbidden to touch the Tree of Knowledge and describes the creation of Eve. Raphael departs.

Book IX Eve persuades Adam to allow her to go off and work on her own. Adam is reluctant, but agrees. Satan finds her alone and tempts her. She eats the fruit and persuades Adam to do the same.

Book X The Son descends to Eden and pronounces doom on Adam and Eve and the Serpent. Satan returns in triumph to Pandemonium. He, 'first in sin', will also be doomed. Sin and Death ascend to Eden, claiming the World as theirs. God foretells their overthrow by the Son. Through his Angels, God effects changes in the elements and the stars so that the Earth becomes susceptible to change and corruption. Adam and Eve repent and ask mercy of God.

Book XI God sends Michael to Eden to show the future to Adam, particularly his hope of Redemption. He shows him a vision of the World's history until the Flood.

Book XII   Michael shows the history of Israel from the Flood
to the coming of Christ, and the subsequent progress of Christi-
anity. He leads Adam and Eve to the gates of Eden, from
which they are gently expelled. They are assured of their ultimate salvation.

Book I, lines 1–75 (pp.49–51)

Milton states his theme in a mighty sentence. Matthew
Arnold, in *On Translating Homer*, commented: 'So chary of a
sentence is he, so resolute not to let it escape him till he has
crowded into it all he can, that it is not until the thirty-ninth
word of the sentence that he will give us the key to it, the word
of action, the verb'. It is characteristic of Milton's mind that
it ranges hugely backwards and forwards in time and space,
and so it is in the span of the opening lines: 'disobedience',
'death', 'woe', 'loss of Eden', 'one greater Man', 'regain the
blissful seat' – the whole vast story is summed up. It is to be an
'adventurous song', of 'things unattempted yet in prose or
rhyme'. To aid him he invokes the *'Heav'nly* Muse', the Holy
Spirit which inspired Moses, the very Spirit which 'moved upon
the face of the waters'. If the Holy Spirit created a structured
universe out of 'the vast abyss' it can help him create order
out of the chaos of his subject.

The second sentence comes home to the *purpose* of his poem
– to 'assert Eternal Providence, / And justify the ways of God
to men'.

This opening is an imitation of the Greek and Latin epics
but also a rejection of them. His poem is to be about Man's
first disobedience, not about the noble deeds of heroes in battle
(cf. 'Arms and the man I sing'). The poem is dedicated to God.

Milton comes to his story. Why did Man fall, transgressing
God's will, 'for one restraint, lords of the world besides'? This
brings us to Satan, who 'trusted to have equalled the most
High' – an absurdly inflated self-contradictory claim. The
word 'Satan' means enemy and tempter. There is emphasis

on Satan's pride and desire for self-glorification. True, there is a perverse grandeur about the lines

> Against the throne and monarchy of God
> Raised impious war in heav'n and battle proud,

but it collapses on 'With vain attempt' as though a trapdoor had been opened beneath him, and he continues throughout the poem to be both heroic and absurd, sometimes together, sometimes alternately. The following three lines re-enact his headlong fall, with no punctuation to break it. Again the self-defeating nature of Satan's crime is emphasized: 'who durst defy th' Omnipotent to arms'.

One of Satan's punishments is the thought of 'lost happiness': he can still appreciate what he has chosen to lose. There follows a description of Hell, not only in physical terms –

> A dungeon horrible on all sides round
> As one great furnace flames –

but also as a place of spiritual deprivation,

> where peace
> And rest can never dwell, hope never comes.

The repeated 'never' is chilling. We are reminded that Hell is largely internal: as Satan says in Book IV, 'my self am Hell'. Hell is being irrecoverably removed from God 'as from the centre thrice to th' utmost pole'. It is essentially deprivation.

It is worth noting that in the last thirty lines of the passage, as throughout Milton, many words are used that are stronger and richer, in their 17th-century usage – when they were closer to their etymological base (generally, not always, Latin) – than they are now: for example, baleful, affliction, dismay, dismal, horrible, doleful. These words have become worn away with use and misuse over the centuries and it is probably impossible now to recover their full force, though a knowledge of Latin often helps.

page 49

mortal Deadly
one greater Man Christ, the second Adam
Heav'nly Muse The invocation of the Muse is in the epic
convention. Milton, however, does not invoke one of the Nine
Muses, but the Muse of sacred song which inspired Moses on
Sinai and David on Zion. Horeb (Oreb) is the whole range of
mountains, Sinai a particular mountain. Moses was supposed to
have prefigured 'the good shepherd' Christ, and is the 'that
shepherd' referred to.
Siloa's brook The Muses frequented the spring and altar of Zeus.
Milton gives the idea a scriptural dress: the Heavenly Muse
haunts the spring that flows by the Temple ('the oracle') of
the Almighty.
Fast by Close by. Siloa was outside Jerusalem.
no middle flight Milton intends to ascend to the highest
Empyrean
th' Aonian mount Helicon, sacred to the Muses
pursues Treats of
O Spirit The Holy Spirit. Milton believed that a great poem can
be written only with the aid of the Holy Spirit.
argument Subject
assert Vindicate

page 50

grand Original
For Because of
what time At the time when
peers Equals
combustion Being consumed by fire
witnessed Showed, testified
darkness visible Gloom in which things are barely visible

page 51

As from the centre thrice to th' utmost pole The distance
of Hell from the Empyrean is equal to three times the distance

from the earth ('the centre') to the utmost pole of the globe or universe.

Book I, lines 84–124 Satan to Beelzebub (pp.51–2)

'Beelzebub' means 'lord of the flies'. The name is ugly and frightful, but also grotesquely comic.

Satan's speech is highly characteristic; he is immediately dramatized in full rhetorical power. The revolt against God was a 'glorious enterprise' – he has the insolence to say this despite their present plight. He forestalls any attack on his leadership by arguing that

> till then who knew
> The force of those dire arms? –

to which rhetorical question the answer, presumably, would be 'Everybody'. He determines not to 'repent or change' since repentance is weakness. It sounds grandly firm-minded, but it is his tragedy that he is incapable of change, unlike Adam and Eve. His 'fixed mind' – is it a sign of greatness or of weakness to be incapable of changing one's mind? – is full of a sense of 'high disdain, from sense of injured merit'. Satan is full of a kind of huge pettiness. He cannot claim to have won the battle, but at least, for what it's worth, he 'shook his throne'. There follows a piece of splendid rhetoric:

> What though the field be lost?
> All is not lost,

which is very Churchillian; but all he has to fall back on is the meanness of 'study of revenge, immortal hate'. The petty sense is at variance with the grand rhythms. Basically, he would rather be in Hell than 'bow and sue for grace': that is, recognize his proper subordination. He will use his experience of failure to be more successful next time. For him, God is a tyrant; so he intends to set up his own tyranny in Hell.

page 51

He with his thunder The account of the battle is in Book III,
lines 392–3 and Book VI, lines 836–8.

page 52

dubious battle The battle lasted three days
That glory never shall his wrath or might / Extort from me
The victor (God) shall never extort from me the glory of my
submission
by fate Satan denies that the angels were created by the
Almighty. He believes that they were 'self-begotten': it is vital to
him to think of himself as self-sufficient. He recognizes Fate, not
the Almighty, as superior.
And this empyreal substance cannot fail The fiery substance
of their forms cannot perish
successful hope Hope of success

Book I, lines 157–91 (pp.52–3)

The endless struggle between good and evil is summed up in:

> If then his providence
> Out of our evil seek to bring forth good,
> Our labour must be to pervert that end,
> And out of good still to find means of evil.

So Satan turns the good of the Garden of Eden to evil; God,
in reply, turns the evil to greater good by sending His Son.
    God's 'ministers of vengeance' have retired: now is their
chance to

> Consult how we may henceforth most offend
> Our Enemy.

page 52

if I fail not If I am not mistaken

page 53

His ministers The good angels
laid Laid to rest, stilled
slip Let slip
offend Strike at, harm

Book I, lines 242–70 (pp.53–4)

Again Satan suffers a moment's homesickness for 'that celestial light', but it soon passes. He accepts that 'farthest from him is best', and claims that God is not superior in reason, merely in power, though by using the words 'right' and 'best' he reveals his own confusion and perhaps gives his case away. With a ringing *Ave atque vale* he bids farewell to the 'happy fields / Where joy for ever dwells' and welcome to the 'Infernal world'. 'Receive thy new possessor' reverberates with the pride of ownership, but we know that the property he has inherited is simply 'mournful gloom' and desolation. He wants to have it all ways at once. His pride in being 'One who brings / A mind not to be changed by place or time' is crass obstinacy rather than true firmness of mind. And, in any case, Satan is always changing: consistency is impossible to him.

'The mind is its own place, and in itself / Can make a heav'n of hell, a hell of heav'n' is a reminder that the 17th century did not think of Hell merely as a physical underground pit. Satan carries Hell round with him wherever he goes; his mind is a pit of darkness. Satan intends us to think, of course, that he can convert Hell into Heaven by mental process, and it may well be true that one man's Hell is another man's Heaven.

There is a perverse heroism in Satan's 'Better to reign in Hell than serve in Heav'n', but, stripped of its neat, clinching finality, the line is absurd. It is a characteristically Satanic device to turn 'serve' into a dirty word.

page 53

change for Take in exchange for

Whom reason hath equalled, force hath made supreme
Satan thinks that the Devils were equal to God in reason, but not
in force. God is seen as a bully, exercising mere power.

page 54

The mind is its own place The idea that Hell, like Heaven,
is not, or not only, a place but a mental state. In Marlowe's
Dr Faustus the Doctor asks, 'Where is the place that men call
Hell?' Mephistopheles replies:

> Hell hath no limits, nor is circumscribed
> In one self place, for where we are is Hell.

all but less than Nearly equal to
oblivious Causing forgetfulness

Book I, lines 283–313 (pp.54–5)

Satan is now presented as a figure of stupendous size: Evil is
traditionally a huge monster. He calls his legions 'who lay en-
tranced, / Thick as autumnal leaves that strow the brooks / In
Vallombrosa'. Dead leaves are an ancient symbol of the dead;
here they lie in a waste of confusion. Milton then shifts the
simile to liken them to Pharaoh's army overwhelmed by the
Red Sea. By comparison with his 'abject' (in both the old and
the modern senses of the word) host, Satan seems indeed a
hero.

page 54

optic glass Telescope
the Tuscan artist Galileo
Fesolè A hill near Florence, where Galileo lived in his later
  years
Valdarno The valley of the Arno, in which Florence lies
ammiral Flag ship

page 55

Nathless Nevertheless
Vallombrosa 'Shady valley': eighteen miles from Florence
sedge Sea-weed
Orion The period between the rising and the setting of the
   constellation Orion was a period of storms
armed Orion, the hunter, appears among the stars as a giant
   with a girdle, sword and club
vexed Disturbed violently
Busiris An Egyptian king, whom Milton identifies with the
   Pharaoh who perished in the Red Sea
Memphian Egyptian
perfidious Because he had given the Israelites leave to go.
the sojourners of Goshen The Israelites
Abject Cast down

Book I, lines 589–669 (pp.55–7)

Satan addresses himself to the task of raising his legions from
their torpor. We are reminded that he is indeed an Archangel,
though 'ruined'. His courage is 'dauntless', however mis-
placed, for great evil cannot be done without courage. He even
feels, momentarily, 'remorse and passion to behold / The fel-
lows of his crime'. Their glory is withered, like great trees
blasted by lightning. Satan's speech is perfectly calculated to
put new heart into them. First, he again protests that their
defeat in the war in Heaven was not *his* fault: indeed, the
whole business was God's fault since God, by concealing his
strength, 'tempted our attempt and wrought our fall'. Now
they know God's strength, they could try again; nevertheless
they would be advised this time to trust to 'fraud or guile'.
Already there is rumour of a new world, inhabited by 'a
generation ... equal to the sons of Heaven'. They could go
there, 'if but to pry' – and if this suggestion makes them sound
too much like Peeping Toms, he follows it with another dose
of rhetoric – 'For this infernal world shall never hold ...' and
ends with the stirring cry, 'War, then war...' But not only

is this not the noblest of cries, it is not even what Satan intends, since he has already come out in favour of spiting God by trying to destroy His newest toy. Satan uses words merely for effect.

The speech is followed by a tremendous salute from 'millions of flaming swords'. The devils hurl 'defiance toward the vault of heav'n' – a grand, easy gesture which costs nothing.

page 55

eclipse Thought to be of evil omen
intrenched Cut into
considerate Thoughtful

page 56

amerced Deprived
yet faithful how they stood How faithfully they still stood
scathed Damaged
blasted Withered by the lightning
event Result
emptied heav'n This is a greatly exaggerated boast
For me ... have lost our hopes Satan swears before all the
   Host of Heaven that their failure was not due to ignoring advice
   or avoiding danger

page 57

state Pomp
Peace is despaired There is no hope of peace
understood Undeclared
Highly With drunken arrogance

Book I, lines 730–51
The rebel angels build their palace (pp.57–8)

The passage begins in genuine wonder at the creative power

of Mulciber, who built Pandemonium: 'his hand was known /
In heav'n by many a tow'red structure high'. Then Milton
turns on him with venom, picturing him 'headlong sent / With
his industrious crew to build in hell'. Creative genius is reduced to mere mechanical skill. This is another example of
the misuse of great talents, such as is shown by Satan himself.

page 57

entered Entered Pandemonium, the meeting-place 'of all the
devils'

page 58

the architect Mulciber or Vulcan, the god of fire and
metalwork, architect of the palaces of the gods
hierarchy, the orders bright The nine orders of angels
Ausonian land Italy
how he fell When Mulciber interfered in a quarrel in Heaven,
Zeus threw him out. The story is a parallel to the fall of the
angels.
engines Contrivances
industrious Working-class; the 'industrious crew' are the people
who work the machines

Book II, lines 11–42 Satan opens the debate (pp.58–9)

Satan's first task is to renew the morale of his followers. He
speaks to them as though they were still angels and makes it
clear that there will be no surrender. His language has an
apparent, though empty, dignity. He claims leadership by
right of seniority, election and merit. Moreover, he claims, he
is safer than God in Heaven: God's subordinates may well envy
Him – Satan judges others by himself – but nobody will envy
Satan, who is most exposed to 'the Thunderer's aim' and con-

demned to 'greatest share of endless pain'. Satan, who is always adept at trying to have it both ways, says that nobody would want *his* job: he is being unselfish, he implies, by accepting it. He throws the meeting open to phony debate. Shall there be 'open war or covert guile'? He has already, in fact, devised his own plan, which Beelzebub will reveal when the moment is ripe.

pages 58–9

I give not heav'n for lost I do not consider Heaven lost

trust themselves to fear no second fate Gain such confidence as not to fear a second defeat

Me though just right ... Yielded with full consent In this tortuous sentence Satan is asserting his right to be their leader. First, he was created their senior in Heaven; second, he was elected; third, he deserves his position because of his prowess in debate and in war; fourth, he has raised them from the lake of fire into Pandemonium, a partial recovery.

page 59

unenvied Unenviable

state Constitution, based on rank. Satan says that envy is understandable in Heaven, but in Hell he who is in the highest position faces the most risks. This absence of envy will be an advantage to them in the forthcoming battle.

the Thunderer God

There are three ways in which the devils can react to their situation. They are put forward by Moloch, Belial and Mammon. Moloch urges outright war; Belial urges submission; Mammon proposes that they make the best of their situation. Mammon's plan receives the overwhelming popular vote until Satan, through Beelzebub, puts forward the idea which promises both peace and revenge.

Book II, lines 51–105 Moloch speaks (pp.59–61)

Moloch plunges straight in, without introduction or subtlety. He is the military man, bluff, staccato, thick-headed: 'Of wiles, / More inexpert, I boast not'. He recognizes that Hell is a 'dark opprobrious den of shame' and wants to get out of it, and he has his 'millions that stand in arms' ready to do the job. He realizes that the attempt may be suicidal, but to be reduced 'to nothing' would be 'happier far / Than miserable to have eternal being'. He knows that he cannot win, but they may 'alarm' the Almighty, 'which', he concludes with ringing absurdity, 'if not victory is yet revenge'. He must be fighting, hurling troops by millions over the top. Anything is better than sitting 'contriving'.

page 59

sentence Opinion, vote
more inexpert Less experienced

page 60

horrid Frightful; bristling
his almighty engine The chariot of wrath with which the Son expelled them from Heaven
for lightning In retaliation for lightning
Tartarean Tartarus was part of the Greek underworld reserved for the guilty dead. Milton frequently mixes Christian with classical allusions.
strange fire The fire of Hell is different from that of Heaven.
Let such bethink them People who think it difficult should remember.
sleepy drench / Of that forgetful lake A 'drench' was a sleeping draught given to animals. The lake of fire in which they had originally been plunged brought forgetfulness.
That in our proper motion we ascend It was natural for spirits to rise

Who but felt Who did not feel?
Insulting Assaulting and exulting
the deep Chaos
event Outcome
Our stronger God
exercise Religious discipline
what doubt we Why do we hesitate?
essential Angelic substance
happier far It is better to be annihilated than to live in misery
  for ever.

page 61

we are at worst / On this side nothing We have reached the
  worst point short of absolute annihilation
proof Experience
fatal Upheld by fate, and so secure. Also deadly.

Book II, lines 119–213 Belial speaks (pp.61–3)

Belial is a good deal more intelligent than Moloch, which is
not difficult. He is suave, orderly, up to a point rational. He
uses the rhetorical device of asking loaded questions and
answering them himself, sometimes piling them one on top of
the other – 'What if ... what if...' and concluding with the
annihilating 'this would be worse'. He mocks Moloch, who
grounds 'his courage on despair'. They cannot win a war, and,
after all, they aren't so badly off as they are, 'Thus sitting,
thus consulting, thus in arms'. They were worse when they
were 'chained on the burning lake'. They must not provoke
God to 'arm again / His red right hand to plague us'. The
vividness with which he describes possible future punishments
shows that his root feeling is fear – perhaps legitimate fear since
he understands all too well how 'He from heav'n's highth / All
these our motions vain sees and derides'. And perhaps, after
all, God will forget about them, in time.

Milton's comment on this, not included in the present selection, is contemptuous:

> Thus Belial with words clothed in reason's garb
> Counselled ignoble ease, and peaceful sloth,
> Not peace.

page 61

urged Put forward as the main argument for
fact Deeds, action. Belial goes on to point out that Moloch has admitted that he cannot win, merely 'revenge'.
scope Limit
watch Guards
obscure Dark
Or could we Or even if we could
th' ethereal mould 'mould' means substance. The Angelic spirits are compounded entirely of fire, which would resist the baser fires of Hell.
we must We should be bound to

page 62

intellectual being Mental existence
rather Instead
Let this be good Even if we supposed, for the sake of argument, that annihilation would be good
Belike No doubt. Belial, of course, is being sarcastic.
impotence Impatience
Wherefore cease we then i.e. those who advise war ask why we should give up the struggle.
amain With all speed
intermitted Temporarily stopped
firmament The roof of Hell

page 63

racking Either driving along, or torturing. Belial is cataloguing the traditional tortures of Hell.

hopeless end No end to hope for
for what can force or guile / With him What can force or
  guile do against him?
motions Plans
To suffer, as to do, / Our strength is equal We are as able to
  suffer and endure as to attack.
Not mind Take no notice
satisfied / With what is punished Satisfied with the
  punishment he has already inflicted on us

Book II, lines 229–83 Mammon speaks (pp.64–5)

'Mammon' means 'wealth'. His advice is materialistic: they
must seek 'our own good from ourselves', 'to none account-
able', 'preferring / Hard liberty before the easy yoke / Of
servile pomp'. They can make the best of things, make 'great
things of small, / Useful of hurtful, prosperous of adverse'.
They can make an imitation Heaven out of Hell. All this
sounds admirable, until we learn how Mammon proposes to
do it – by magnificent and expensive architecture, for 'what
can Heaven show more?' Mammon believes that all misery
can be removed by the spending of money and the white heat
of technological revolution.

  To Mammon, as to Satan, the idea of 'subjection' is repel-
lent. He pours scorn on the idea of humility, on Heaven's
'warbled hymns' and 'forced hallelujahs'. Service, to him, is
servility. So he mocks the essence of Heaven while seeking to
emulate its superficialities.

page 64

Him to unthrone we then ... as vain / The latter We shall
  only dethrone God when all order collapses. We cannot hope for
  that, so we cannot hope to dethrone God.
Ambrosial Ambrosia is dervied from a word meaning 'immortal'
  which the Greeks used for the food and drink of their gods. It is
  a symbol of incorruptibility.

by leave obtained / Unacceptable Even if we were allowed to
  have it, we do not want to be in a state of servitude again.
Our own good from ourselves Make life bearable by using our
  own resources
recess Remote place of retirement

page 65

desert Sterile
Wants not Does not lack
elements Natural environments
sensible Feeling
Compose Arrange, adapt ourselves to

Book II, lines 310–80 Beelzebub speaks (pp.65–7)

Mammon's speech has met with popular approval. Now is the
moment for Beelzebub to produce the master-plan. First, he
demolishes the others' proposals: 'What sit we here projecting
peace or war?' Both are impossible to them. But there is an
'easier enterprise'. They should attack the 'new race called
Man', which may not be well defended. 'This would surpass
/ Common revenge' and be infinitely better than 'Hatching
vain empires'.

  'The bold design', we are later told, 'Pleased mightily those
infernal states'. It is an essentially mean plan: they cannot hurt
God, so they will vandalize His garden. It is some consolation
to the miserable to make others miserable, so

>   his darling sons
>   Hurled headlong to partake with us, shall curse
>   Their frail original, and faded bliss,
>   Faded so soon.

The last words sadistically mock the pathos of Man's fall.
Beelzebub envies Man's happiness, so he must destroy it.

page 65

style Title
the popular vote Beelzebub judges by the applause for
  Mammon.
doomed Decreed

page 66

What sit we? Why do we sit here?
projecting In the 17th century the word 'project' suggested
  something fraudulent or absurd
determined Finished
foiled Frustrated
stripes Whipping
to our power To the limit of our power
reluctance Resistance
Nor will occasion want Opportunity will not be lacking
ancient and prophetic fame Long-rife rumour about the future

page 67

attempted Attacked
left / To their defence who hold it Left to be defended by
  Man
puny Little and weak, but also, by derivation from the French
  puis né 'born since'
darling Favourite
original God, or Adam
Advise Consider
Hatching In a parody of the Creator

Book II, lines 430–66
Satan alone dares the voyage to this new world (pp.67–8)

In a passage omitted from this selection, Beelzebub proposes
the dramatic question,

> whom shall we send
> In search of this new world, whom shall we find
> Sufficient?

He paints a terrifying (and not exaggerated) picture of the perils involved:

> who shall tempt with wandering feet
> The dark unbottomed infinite abyss
> And through the palpable obscure find out
> His uncouth way, or spread his airy flight
> Upborne with indefatigable wings
> Over the vast abrupt, ere he arrive
> The happy isle . . .

Not surprisingly, 'all sat mute, / Pondering the danger with deep thoughts'. This gives Satan his great dramatic moment. He rises to his feet, 'with monarchal pride / Conscious of highest worth', to offer himself.

Satan re-emphasizes the dangers that will face him as a prelude to

> But I should ill become this throne, O Peers . . .
> if aught . . .
> Of difficulty or danger could deter
> Me from attempting.

The emphasis on 'Me' is superb, the climax of his whole contrived dramatic scene, and it is fitting that it is the personal pronoun that should receive so much weight. Satan begins and ends with 'Me'. After a little flattery – he calls the devils, ludicrously, 'Terror of heav'n, though fall'n – he urges them to entertain themselves as best they can while he is away, and escapes before anybody can have the opportunity to offer to share the glory of the 'enterprise' with him: they would have to be refused, but would acquire some cheap glory.

page 67

convex Vault

unessential Non-existent
abortive Monstrously unnatural; anybody entering Chaos may
  be reduced to non-existence.
moment importance
Wherefore do I assume ... High honoured sits How could I
  accept kingship if I did not accept the risks which accompany it?
intend Consider
intermit Neglect
coasts Regions

Book II, lines 521–628 (pp.68–71)

The devils disperse to entertain themselves. Key words are
'wand'ring', 'perplex'd', 'restless'. They organize games,
peaceful and warlike; they amuse themselves by tearing up
rocks and hills, venting frustration in violent activity; they
make beautiful music, so beautiful that 'the harmony / Suspended hell', but all they have to sing about is 'Their own
heroic deeds and hapless fall'; others philosophize about
'providence, foreknowledge, will and fate / And found no end,
in wand'ring mazes lost'.

  Other devils investigate the geography of Hell, which gives
Milton the opportunity to pile up lists of all the horrors which
mankind through history has attributed to Hell. But wherever
they go, whatever they do, they find 'No rest'; it is 'A universe
of death ... Where all life dies, death lives'. Hell is full of
'Chimeras dire'; all is fantasy, illusion and nightmarish paradox.

page 68

ranged Arranged in ranks
several Different

page 69

sublime Uplifted
Olympian games on Pythian fields The Greek games held at Olympia every four years and at Delphi. They were held in honour of Apollo, the Pythian god.
shun the goal Steer closely round the post in a chariot race
fronted brigades Opposing teams, ready for a tournament
van Vanguard
Prick Ride.
welkin Sky
Typhoean Typhoeus' name meant 'whirlwind'
Alcides Hercules. The story to which the following lines refer is briefly this: returning home from conquest in Oechalia, Hercules sent for a robe in which to make a thank-offering to Zeus. His wife sent a robe dipped in a love-potion to make him faithful to her. It was poisonous and stuck to his skin. In agony, he threw Lichas, who had brought the robe, into the sea.
virtue Strength
partial Prejudiced
Suspended Held rapt
took Enchanted

page 70

gross Dense, compact
clime Region
baleful Sorrowful
Styx The rivers of Hell are chiefly derived from the *Aeneid*. The meaning of the names is referred to in Milton's descriptions.
flood River
ruin seems / Of ancient pile The hail looks like the ruins of an old building
that Serbonian bog Lake Serbonis (now dried up) in Egypt. When sand blew into it, it looked like a desert. A Persian army marched in and sank.

page 71

frore Freezing
harpy-footed Harpies were hideous, winged creatures with
  hooked claws
Furies Avenging goddesses
revolutions Seasons
starve Die
sound Estuary
fate withstands It is impossible for them
Medusa One of the three Gorgons. She was so terrible to behold
  that anyone who looked at her turned to stone.
wight Man
Tantalus He was punished in Hades with a raging thirst while
  at the same time being placed in the middle of a lake whose
  waters receded when he tried to drink
prodigious Unnatural
Hydras The Hydra was a snake with nine heads
Chimeras The Chimera was a three-headed female monster: it
  stands for illusion and fantasy.

Book III, lines 56–134
God sees Satan flying towards the newly created world
(pp.72–4)

Here Milton introduces God for the first time. The verse to
begin with is noble and eloquent, but simple, a happy change
from the convolutions and paradoxes so appropriate in the
previous passage. The Garden of Eden, too, is introduced
simply as 'the happy garden', with 'our two first parents ...
Reaping immortal fruits of joy and love', – though the word
'fruit' casts its shadow forward. Milton does not scorn the
use of the obvious, even trite – as, for instance, when Adam's
slack hand lets fall the garland when Eve returns to him after
the Fall, or when, at the very end, Adam and Eve 'with
wand'ring steps and slow / Through Eden took their solitary
way'. These moments remind us that, despite all its elabora-
tions, the poem is based on certain great simplicities.

The dialogue which follows is less happy. It was dangerous and difficult to make The Word speak, and at times The Word seems unnecessarily wordy. It is surely unnecessary for Him to explain how Man will fall and how it will be his own fault, how the Tree of Knowledge was a test of Man's obedience and how this can be reconciled with God's own foreknowledge. For one thing, God tends to sound self-justificatory and even petulant – 'they themselves decreed / Their own revolt, not I'. Secondly, is it really necessary for God to explain all this to the Son, who surely would know it already? Is it not really Milton who is trying to explain and justify, and, if so, is this the place for such a kind of writing? Thirdly, Milton draws attention to the difficult theological and philosophical problems which lie behind the poem, and the reader may well not accept the explanations, even though they are put into God's mouth. It is important, of course, to realize that Adam and Eve had free will and fell through their own fault, though it is difficult to understand how it could be so since God is both omniscient and omnipotent: if we try to understand the matter we are likely to become, like the devils, 'in wand'ring mazes lost'. It is something of a relief to come to the end of God's speech and find him asserting that 'mercy first and last shall brightest shine'.

page 72

empyrean Heaven
the sanctities The divine beings
his sight The sight of him
the gulf Chaos
Firm land imbosomed without firmament Viewed from outside, the Earth seemed to be a solid mass of land, without sky
Uncertain It being uncertain
Transports Both literal and metaphorical
Wide interrupt With its wide division between Heaven and Hell

page 73

assay Attempt
Glozing Flattering in a deceptive and lying way
the sole command i.e. not to eat from the forbidden tree
Ingrate Ungrateful
had served necessity, / Not me If man and the angels had had
  no free will they would have served necessity, not me.

page 74

The first sort The angels
suggestion Temptation

Book III, lines 144–216 (pp.74–6)

The Son, with his insistence that 'men should find grace', is
naturally a warmer and more sympathetic figure than the
more authoritarian Father. The Father, in his reply, again out-
lines one of the tangles of theology: 'Man shall not quite be
lost, but saved who will, / Yet not of will in him, but grace
in me'. Has Man after the Fall got free will or has he not? Is
the doctrine of Election reconcilable with that of Free Will?
God begins to look disconcertingly Calvinist. Moreover, the
idea of Atonement as 'rigid satisfaction, death for death' seems
crude as a theory until The Son gives us a foretaste of God's
love in action.

page 74

return i.e. to Hell

page 75

My Word The Son is referred to in the New Testament as 'The
  Word'.
effectual might The power by which God effected His will
lapsed temporarily lost
exorbitant Excessive
mortal Deadly
of peculiar grace / Elect above the rest The doctrine of
  Predestination

page 76

Affecting Seeking to win. In Book IX the Serpent temps Eve with the promise of Godhead.

sacred and devote Utterly doomed

mortal ... mortal A pun. The first 'mortal' means 'subject to death'; the second means 'deadly'.

Book III, lines 227–65
The Son offers himself as a ransom for man (pp.76–7)

The difficult theorizing is left behind: the Son turns it into a practical matter. He will go to earth, die, rise again, descend into Hell, slay death, 'Then with the multitude of my re-deemed / Shall enter Heaven'. It is a heroic programme of action, surpassing and checkmating Satan. And Satan's 'heroism' was motivated by spite; the Son's is motivated by love.

page 76

passed Pledged

unprevented Unanticipated. Grace comes before man has prayed for it.

meet Fitting

page 77

maugre In spite of

ruin Hurl down

Book IV, lines 58–113
Satan, nearing Eden, questions himself (pp.77–9)

Satan's confusions reveal themselves as he sees the beauty of the Garden. It is characteristic of him that he should first be tortured by a sense of the beauty and goodness of what he has lost: it is the same when he first sees Eve. We – and he – are reminded that he is a lost archangel. The evil in him is momentarily suspended before 'the hot hell that always in him burns' takes over again. He acknowledges that his will 'Chose freely what it now so justly rues'. He carries Hell about with him: 'myself am Hell'. Part of the Hell is that he wants to relent, but cannot, since the condition of pardon is unconditional surrender, and this is impossible since 'Disdain forbids me'. Moreover, he would lose face in the eyes of the other devils, to whom he promised the impossible, 'to subdue / Th' Omnipotent'. The only thing left for him, then, is to press on in the course he has chosen, declaring 'Evil, be thou my good'. But he knows the evil to be evil and knows himself 'only supreme / In misery'. There are interesting points of comparison here with Macbeth and other Shakespearian hero-villains.

page 78

abide Suffer for
advanced Raised to eminence
By act of grace By asking pardon
violent Extorted by compulsion

page 79

more than half perhaps He rules Hell and hopes to rule the world

Book IV, lines 205–325 (pp.79–82)

In great luxuriant sentences Milton describes 'Nature's whole wealth' in the Garden before the Fall. 'Nature boon / Poured forth profuse on hill and dale and plain', satisfying all the senses. Even the pagan world is at home there – universal Pan, the Graces, the Hours 'Led on th' eternal spring' in the harmony of a dance, the symbol of order and unity.

We are made aware, however, of the contrasting disharmony that is to come; the Tree of Knowledge is mentioned –

> Proserpine gathering flow'rs,
> Herself a fairer flow'r, by gloomy Dis
> Was gathered, which cost Ceres all that pain
> To seek her through the world

– a moving reminder of Eve and of the pain which the Fall introduced into the world; and 'the Fiend' is there, seeing 'undelighted all delight'.

Indeed, Satan's presence is mentioned immediately before the description of Adam and Eve 'God-like erect, with native honour clad / In naked majesty'. 'The image of their glorious maker' still shines in them because they accept their place in Creation; they live in 'filial freedom'. Their relations with each other are those accepted by contemporary thought: 'He for God only, she for God in him' is not Milton's male chauvinism, but a commonplace of the time. Milton emphasizes their sexuality; they are proud of their nakedness; there is neither prurience nor shame; Adam exercises 'gentle sway' and Eve yields with 'sweet reluctant amorous delay'. They embody what we have now lost, man's 'happiest life / Simplicity and spotless innocence', and their behaviour is contrasted with their behaviour immediately after the Fall.

page 79

Eden stretched her line / From Auran eastward Eden lay in Syria and Mesopotamia. Auran is in Syria, south of Damascus: Selencia, once capital of Western Asia, is near modern Baghdad.
blooming Bearing in quantity
shaggy Because covered in trees

page 80

nether Lower
wand'ring Wandering through

sapphire fount Source the colour of sapphire
crisped Rippling
error Wandering
nice Precise. A verb such as 'planted' needs to be supplied.
curious knots Elaborately laid-out plots
boon Beautiful
Imbrowned Darkened
view Appearance
gums Aromatic resins, such as myrrh and balm
amiable Lovely
Hesperian fables true, / If true, here only If the stories of
the apples of the Hesperides were true, they were true here and
nowhere else.
lawns Glades
irriguous Well-watered
umbrageous Shady

page 81

apply Practise or add
airs Means breezes, but there is a suggestion that birdsong and
breezes become one in natural harmony
Pan The god of all Nature
the Graces The three goddesses who personified the joys of life
the Hours Goddesses personifying the seasons of the year
Led on Carrying on the metaphor of the dance
Not that fair field / Of Enna Enna, in Sicily, was the place
where Proserpine was carried off to the underworld by Pluto
(Dis), unknown to Ceres, her mother
nor that sweet grove / Of Daphne by Orontes On the
Orontes, near Antioch, was a grove named Daphne, watered
by a spring called the Castalian spring
strive Compete
nor that Nyseian isle A king of Libya named Ammon married
Rhea; by a girl called Amalthea he had a son, Dionysus, or
Bacchus, the god of wine. Ammon hid his son on a
Mediterranean island at Nysa, which is surrounded by the river
Triton, to protect him from Rhea. Nysa was a place of great
beauty. The Libyans identified Ammon with Jove.

florid Ruddy, as befits the god of wine

Nor where Abassin kings ... The mountain of Amara was supposed to be a day's journey high. The Emperor of Abyssinia is supposed to have shut up his sons there, to prevent them from sedition. It was a beautiful place, supposed by some to have been the site of Paradise.

Ethiop line The equator

sanctitude Holiness

page 82

front Forehead

hyacinthine Probably deep brown

wanton Unrestrained

dishonest Unchaste

Book IV, lines 340–94 (pp. 82–4)

The animals are playfully described in their unfallen state, the lion and the kid playing together, the elephant with its 'lithe proboscis' giving amusement as the local clown and an example of the Almighty's sense of humour; but again the serpent is among those present.

Satan, seeing Adam and Eve in their innocence, becomes a rather stagey villain as he gloats over the insecurity of their happiness and weeps a few crocodile tears before urging 'public reasons just' – i.e. political necessity – for his attack on them. He is making the necessary descent from the heroic figure of Books I and II to the serpentine tempter of Books IX and X.

page 83

ramped Sprang

ounces Lynxes

Insinuating Winding itself into folds

Gordian twine An intricate knot

His braided train His twisted, interlaced body

Or bedward ruminating Chewing the cud as they went to bed

th' ocean isles The Atlantic
failed speech Speech that had failed him
for so happy Considering how happy they are
forlorn Defenceless

page 84

for him who wronged Instead of him who wronged
public reason just ... compels me now Public reasons – the
  good of honour and empire – as well as revenge compel me to
  conquer this new world.

Book IV, lines 411–91 Adam to Eve (pp.84–6)

In the course of their dialogue Adam and Eve reveal the
existence of the Tree of Knowledge, and that 'God hath pronounced it death to taste that tree'. They thus, unknowingly,
give the listening Satan the weapon he needs. It may be that
Adam has an unhealthy prepossession with the prohibited tree.

   Adam's speech is dignified, and he is happy in the enjoyment
of the garden, Eve and the beneficence of God. The work
of tending the garden is delightful.

   Eve's account of her experiences after her creation emphasize
her dependence, her innocence, and perhaps her potential
vanity as she admires herself in the water: these are qualities
which are to contribute to her downfall.

page 85

possess Occupy
easy Easy to keep (and easy to break)
odds Superiority

page 86

stays Waits for
platan Plane-tree
individual Inseparable

Book IV, lines 502–35 (p.87)

Satan has now acquired a mean malevolence, a 'jealous leer malign'. He cannot bear to see other people happy, 'Imparadised in one another's arms'. The devils in Hell, it seems, suffer from frustrated sexual desire. Hearing of the Tree of Knowledge, he thinks instantly of the plan for their downfall, resenting, on Man's behalf, any limitation, however small, on their freedom. By the end of the speech he is a melodramatic villain, asking to be hissed off the stage.

page 87

A chance but chance my lead It is a chance that chance may lead me

Book V, lines 224–45
God sends Raphael to warn Adam (p.88)

God sends Raphael to warn Adam 'to beware / He swerve not, too secure', and to warn him that the attempt will be made by 'deceit and lies'. But God knows that Adam will fall, so Raphael's warning can only make Adam more guilty and less able to find excuse.

page 88

secure Implies, as often, a false sense of security, resulting in carelessness

Book VI, lines 853–904
Raphael tells Adam of the revolt in heaven and how the Son drove out the rebels (pp.88–90)

The passage energetically describes the Son's victory over the

rebels, their descent into Hell and the Son's triumphant return
to God's right hand.

page 89

ruining Falling
Her i.e. Hell's

Book VII, lines 516–47
Raphael describes the creation of this world and of man
pp.90–91

This passage consists mostly of a direct transcription of the
book of Genesis. When Milton alters it, to make it fit the blank
verse line, he somewhat spoils the Bible's direct simplicity. The
passage ends with a further warning against Satan's wiles.

page 90

Express Exact
for race For the reproduction of the species

Book VIII, lines 460–89
Adam tells Raphael of his first meeting with Eve (pp.91–2)

Adam's passionate account of Eve's creation and his love for
her goes far to explain why he later chooses to fall and die
with her. There is 'heav'n in her eye', and his language hardly
falls short of idolatry.

page 91

Abstract Abstracted
cordial Belonging to the heart

Book IX, lines 152–78
Satan, in Paradise, enters the serpent and
induces Eve to eat of the apple (pp.92–3)

Satan, who fell from a sense of 'injured merit', is absurdly
conscious of the importance of hierarchy: he thinks it an
'indignity' for angels to be used as earth's guards. Yet he wraps
himself in mist and pries into bushes looking for the serpent
so that he can take on the serpent's form. This is Satan's
'incarnation'; he uses the world himself. A 'foul descent'! He
recognizes, moreover, that revenge 'back on itself recoils', like
a gun backfiring. Judging others by himself, he thinks that God
created Man out of spite, and ends with spitting blatancy,
'Spite then with spite is best repaid'. This is the hollowness
which is at the heart of all his grand speeches.

page 92

world The universe
flaming ministers The fiery cherubim
hap Chance
erst Formerly
Who aspires Whoever aspires
obnoxious Vulnerable
reck Care
Since higher I fall short Satan cannot aim at heaven, so he
  aims at Man.

page 93

son of despite According to Satan, Man is the product of God's
  spite towards him

Book IX, lines 445–70 (p.93)

The passage begins with a long simile describing the pleasure

Satan feels when he sees Eve. She is, in the common phrase, 'a breath of fresh air' after the stink which Satan carries around with him. Satan is like a man going out into the country after being 'long in populous city pent', smelling the grass and admiring the passing 'fair virgin'. There is likeness in the simile, but also difference, since Satan's intention is rape. For a moment 'the Evil One abstracted stood / From his own evil', but the emphatic 'But' of 'But the hot hell that always in him burns' is inevitable, and Satan becomes himself again, burning with envy.

page 93

annoy Pollute
tedded Spread out to dry
kine Cattle
for her Because of her
plat Plot
air / Of gesture Her appearance when she made a gesture
rapine Satan comes to rape, but is 'raped' by Eve's beauty.
Stupidly Dumbly

Book IX, lines 523–631 (pp.93–7)

Satan, disguised as the serpent, approaches Eve bowing and 'fawning', dumb with an admiration which is only partly assumed. He begins with flattery, in the elaborate language of courtly love. 'Thee all things living gaze on'. What a pity that there are not more people to admire her! She should be – he is planting an important idea – 'A goddess among gods adored and served / By angels numberless'.

'Into the heart of Eve his words made way' – the phrase suggests insidiousness. She asks how the brute can speak. Satan is a quick opportunist, and also the father of lies. He produces the lie on which the rest of his plan depends: he has eaten the fruit of a tree – he doesn't yet (it might have put Eve on her guard) say *which* tree. He describes the fruit in mouth-watering terms, attributing to it his powers of reason and speech, and ends with more flattery. By now he is offering her 'worship'.

Eve, although she has been warned by Adam of the dangers of going off by herself, is 'unwary', perhaps thrown off her guard by the flattery. She is now 'Empress'. Her 'Lead then' may well carry an ironic echo of 'Lead us not into temptation'.

page 94

turret crest Satan has adopted the form of a snake
enamelled Glossy, multi-coloured
Of her attention gained That he had gained her attention
Organic, or impulse of vocal air Satan spoke either by using his tongue or by using the vibrations of the air
sovran Supreme
thy awful brow, more awful thus retired Eve's beauty is awe-inspiring – the more so because so few see it
admired Wondered at – a strong word in the 17th century
rude Primitive
glozed Flattered and deceived
proem Prologue
The latter I demur I do not believe the latter point – that animals lack 'human sense'

page 95

How cam'st thou speakable of mute? How did you come to be able to speak after being dumb?
brutal kind The animals
abject Base
aught Anything
Grateful Pleasant
fennel Supposed to be a snake's favourite food
tend their play Continue to play (rather than eating)

to degree / Of reason To such an extent that I acquired reason

Wanted not long, though to this shape retained I did not lack speech for long, though I kept a serpent's shape.

capacious Large

middle The space between heaven and earth

Semblance Appearance

spirited Inhabited by the spirit of Satan

thy overpraising leaves in doubt / The virtue of that fruit You praise me so much that I doubt whether the fruit has really given you powers of reason.

incorruptible Nature was incorruptible until the Fall

Grow up to their provision Grow in numbers until there are enough to enjoy all that Nature provides

bearth Fruit

ready Near at hand

Fast Near

blowing Blossoming

conduct Guidance

Book IX, lines 643–7 (p.97)

Satan is now, plainly, a 'snake'. He 'glisters' – and 'all that that glisters is not gold'. Eve is 'our credulous mother': that is, she should be protective but she brings about 'all our woe'.

The questions arises, to what extent was Eve *responsible* for her credulousness? Credulousness may be only another name for trusting innocence, and she did not lose her innocence until she had eaten of the Tree of Knowledge. Perhaps; but in the end her sin was disobedience. God said, 'Thou shalt not' and she disobeyed. She makes it clear that she understands perfectly well that 'of this tree we may not taste or touch'; she even repeats God's precise instruction, in its brevity and finality, word for word.

Satan, now 'The Tempter', puts on a 'new part'. He is always a good actor. The new part is that of an advocate, urging the wrongs done to man.

page 97

dire Deadly
fraud Crime and deception
tree / Of prohibition Forbidden tree
Fruitless An obvious pun. Their journey has been fruitless because Eve is forbidden to eat the fruit.
The credit of whose virtue rest with thee You must remain the sole witness of the fruit's power.
Sole daughter of his voice God's only command
his wrong The wrong done to man (being denied the right to eat from the tree)
New part puts on Begins to play a new part

Book IX, lines 678–785 (pp. 98–101)

Satan's arguments are complex and, when disentangled, contradictory, and Eve does not allow herself the time, and has not the guile, to disentangle them. Satan argues (a) that they will not die; the fruit gives 'life / To knowledge'. He has proved this by himself eating from the tree. This is a lie, and in any case the prohibition presumably did not apply to serpents. (b) Eating the apple is a 'petty trespass'. So it is, in itself; but the tree exists only as a test of their obedience and a guarantee of their free will. (c) They will impress God by their courage in disobeying him, which will show 'dauntless virtue'. This is an essentially Satanic attitude, which could be used to justify any criminal act. The Satanic pride is to think of himself as an independent creature, when he is in fact dependent for his very existence on God, and he wants to infect Eve with the same illusion. (d) What is death, anyway? (e) The tree will produce a 'happier life', knowing both good and evil. (f) It would be unjust of God to punish them for such a trivial offence (or such 'dauntless virtue' – Satan is again having it both ways) and God cannot contradict his own nature by being unjust; therefore he cannot be threatening to punish them for it. (Yes; but an alternative conclusion might be that the offence was not trivial.) (g) All God wants to do is to keep them 'low and ignorant'; but if they eat they will be 'as gods', promoted in the hierarchy as the Serpent claims to have been. (h) Perhaps by 'dying' God simply means that they will cease to be human and become gods. (i) What are gods, anyway? They are useless. Unlike the earth, they produce nothing. (j) Anyway, what is wrong with wanting to know? If everything belongs to God, then what is the harm in the knowledge the tree will bring? (k) Perhaps God is envious and wants to keep them in their place. And there are many other arguments, he says, which he has not time to mention.

'The Tree of Knowledge', of course, is a difficult concept, and Satan takes full advantage of the fact to confuse Eve. The story of the Fall was originally intended to account for the ascent of man from ignorance to knowledge: the tree of knowledge was a symbol of the arts of civilization, which may be a blessing or a curse, though they were unnecessary to man in his unfallen state – he did not need fire in a world where there was a perpetual, temperate spring. Christian theologians, however, whom Milton followed, regarded the story as an explanation of human wickedness, not human science. According to St Augustine, the tree was called 'the tree of the knowledge of good and evil', 'to signify the consequence of their discovering both what good they would experience if they kept the prohibition and what evil if they transgressed it'.

The best way of understanding what is meant is to look at the consequences of eating the apple; and, when all is said and done, the prohibition is clear and unambiguous, and from an unambiguous source.

The serpent's words 'Into her heart too easy entrance won'. Moreover, the mouth-watering smell of the fruit wakes 'an eager appetite'. Like her successors, she finds the fruit the more attractive because it has been forbidden. She accepts the Satanic interpretation of 'knowledge of good and evil' by persuading herself that it cannot be evil to know, to be wise: 'such prohibitions bind not'. The fruit becomes 'the cure of all' – but the Latin 'cura' means 'care'. She eats. Her hand slips up to the tree almost as if it were out of control. Nature responds with a groan, since Nature itself is fallen.

page 98

science Knowledge
deemed however wise However wise they may be thought to be
To knowledge In addition to knowledge
virtue Courage
denounced Proclaimed
Of good, how just? How can it be good to punish you for wanting to acquire a knowledge of good?
Not just, not God; not feared then, nor obeyed If God is not just, then he is not God, and so is not to be feared or obeyed.
I of brute human, ye of human gods As I, by eating the apple, have become human (internally), so you will become gods.

page 99

Human Humanity
participating Sharing
On our belief To make us believe
Them nothing I see that the gods produce nothing.
If they all things If they created all things, then who put the knowledge of good and evil in this tree?
Impart Show
humane Human
replete Filled
impregned Impregnated
to her seeming It seemed to her
inclinable Inclining
assay Trial

page 100

elocution Power of speech
sure Surely
In plain Plainly
after-hands Restrictions after we have eaten the fruit. By the use of 'we' Eve seems to be assuming that Adam, too, will eat the fruit.
author unsuspect The serpent is the first to eat the fruit and cannot be suspected of fraud since he is willing to share the secret of the good which has befallen him.
rather what know to fear How can I know what is to be feared as long as I am ignorant of good and evil?

Book IX, lines 811–33 (pp.101)

The apple seems to have affected Eve's rational powers. She tries to persuade herself that God may not have seen, since He is busy and lives a long way off. He becomes 'Our great Forbidder, safe with all his spies / About him', which is a very Satanic view of God.

Next, she faces the problem of what to do about Adam. Shall she tell him, allowing him to partake 'full happiness'? But if she keeps the secret to herself this will give her 'the odds of knowledge', so she may become his superior. 'Inferior who is free?' is another Satanic position. But what if she *does* die? Adam will marry another Eve – 'A death to think'. So it is ironically out of love for him – genuine love, but with that admixture of possessiveness and selfishness which is perhaps inevitable after the Fall – that she determines that Adam shall die too.

page 101

in what sort How
odds Advantage
wants Is lacking
I extinct When I am dead

Eve returns to Adam, bringing the apple (pp. 101–3)

Eve speaks 'with countenance blithe' – 'but in her cheek distemper flushing glowed'. The distemper is perhaps caused by a kind of drunkenness induced by the apple, but it is also the result of a new dislocation in her whole personality. 'Hast thou not wondered, Adam, at my stay?' perfectly captures her air of assumed innocence, mixed with embarrassment. The tree, she says, will not kill them, though she has already decided that Adam shall die too. She only did it, she says, for him. Her speech is full of an unreal, almost hysterical happiness.

Adam is 'astonied'. The garland he has prepared for her slips from his hand, 'and all the faded roses shed'. Roses fade only in a fallen world, and Eve herself is a faded rose. The rose now is a symbol of transience as well as of love.

Adam does not reproach her: reproaches come *after* he has fallen. She is still 'fairest of creation', but now 'defaced, deflow'red'. The human countenance has lost much of the stamp of the image of God. But Adam has no inward conflict before he decides 'with thee / Certain my resolution is to die'. He cannot live without her: 'the link of Nature' draws him. His expression of love is simple and moving: 'Bone of my bone thou art'.

page 102

Of danger tasted Dangerous to taste
such With such a taste
correspond i.e. to correspond with what the serpent has
 experienced
erst Once
dilated Expanded
lot Fate
Disjoin Divide
distemper A disproportion of the 'humours' which determined

man's temperament. When they were perfectly mixed, man
would live for ever.
Astonished Thunderstruck
horror chill A cold shudder

page 103

defaced Disfigured
deflow'red Violated
devote Cursed
afford Supply

Book IX, lines 997–1059 (pp. 103–5)

Adam ate the apple

                not deceived,
But fondly overcome with female charm.

Eve was deceived: Adam was not. He fell because he loved
Eve so much – or too much. Strictly, he preferred a lesser good
– Eve – to a greater good – God. We must sympathize with
him, even, perhaps, admire him. When Evil comes into the
world Man is put in the position where whatever he does is
wrong. Milton wastes no time on useless moralizing: nor
should we.

The consequences follow immediately. Reason is clouded as
they 'swim in mirth'; they 'fancy that they feel / Divinity
within them'; Adam becomes 'lascivious'; 'in lust they burn',
and lust is very different from love, more simply appetitive.
Adam's speech is smart and leering. He *seizes* her hand and
leads her to a shady bank. Eve is no longer modest; she is
'nothing loth'. Milton is not wholly condemnatory of their
love-making: it is 'of their mutual guilt the seal', but also 'the
solace of their sin'. But it wearies them and the sleep that
follows is unquiet and unrefreshing. When they wake they
have lost their 'native righteousness' and their nakedness is
now shameful. Sex has lost its simplicity.

page 103

fondly Foolishly
iterate Repeat
that So that

page 104

operation Effect
dalliance Love-play
elegant Refined in taste
of sapience no small part Good taste is an important part of wisdom.
purveyed Provided food for
For this one tree Instead of this one tree
As meet is As is fitting
bounty Gift. Eve seems more beautiful than ever since she ate from the tree.
toy Caress
nothing loth Not unwilling

page 105

unkindly Unnatural
conscious This may mean 'inspired by conscience'.
shadowed Protected

Book X, lines 103–208
God sends his Son to judge the transgressors (pp.105–8)

Adam and Eve are hiding: before the Fall they had gone joyfully and openly to meet their celestial visitors. The Son cross-examines them. Of course, he already knows the answers to the questions he asks them, but he has to get a confession of guilt from them as the first step in their regeneration. Now 'Love was not in their looks, either to God / Or to each other'. Adam finds it difficult to give a straight answer to the Son's questions. He worries aloud about accusing Eve, but in the process he does, in fact, accuse her and attempts to excuse himself, arguing not only that it was Eve's fault but also that it was God's fault for making her 'so divine / That from her hand I could suspect no ill'.

The Son replies with the pertinent question, 'Was she thy God?' and distinguishes between love and subjection. Instead of governing Eve, he has made her his God.

Eve, by contrast, makes no excuses.

The Son proceeds to judgment. First, the serpent. Hidden in the curse is a prophecy, which Adam and Eve do not understand, of the Devil's ultimate defeat after the Crucifixion, which Milton reinforces by references to the Old Testament. Then Eve's curse, then Adam's, taken straight from Genesis.

In the passage which follows this (omitted in this selection) the Son clothes them, not just outwardly, but inwardly, with righteousness. We are specifically reminded of Christ washing his disciples' feet. The work of redemption has begun.

page 105

wont Accustomed
discount'nanced Shame-faced
perturbation Excessive passion
revile Reviling
still Always

page 106

devolved Shifted on to
Before his voice i.e. rather than God's voice
real With a suggestion of royalty
Were such as under government well seemed Her gifts were good as long as she remained under Adam's authority.

page 107

in few In few words

the end / Of his creation The purpose of his creation
Spoiled Despoiled

Book XI, lines 423–70
Michael is sent to reveal future things to Adam,
and then to lead Adam and Eve out of Paradise (pp.108–9)

Michael shows the consequences of Adam's sin on 'the whole
included race' by showing the murder of Abel by Cain. A large
part of Adam's pain and guilt is the misery he has brought
on his successors. Michael, however, is able to suggest a life
beyond death in which justice is done.

excepted Banned
tilth Tilled land
sord Surface
Unculled Not carefully picked out

page 109

inwards Inner parts
More terrible at th' entrance than within Dying is more
  terrible than death.

Book XII, lines 606–49 (pp.110–11)

These are the last, moving and memorable, lines of the poem.
Adam and Eve are reconciled to each other. Eve, though conscious that 'all by me is lost', is sustained by the thought that
'By me the Promised Seed shall all restore'. She is now 'our
mother Eve', the credulousness forgotten. Paradise, 'the innocent garden', is now uninhabitable for them as 'torrid heat
/ Began to parch that temperate clime'. As they leave, they
look back to Paradise, 'so late their happy seat'. For a
moment, but only for a moment, they weep 'Some natural
tears'. Then they set out, in pioneering spirit, to the new
world with Providence to guide them. They are together,

'hand in hand', but also solitary as all human beings are solitary. It is an appropriately sadly happy ending.

page 110

fixed station Post of watching
marish Marsh
in front advanced Raise on high, like a flag
vapour Heat
adust Scorched

page 111

subjected Lying below
brand Sword

Questions on Paradise Lost

1 In what ways is Milton's poem similar to Greek and Latin epics and in what ways is it deliberately different?

2 How does Milton picture Hell in *Paradise Lost*? Do you think his picture is successful?

3 What are the main characteristics of Satan in Milton's portrayal of him?

4 Does Milton avoid making Satan too heroic a figure, and by what means does he try to avoid doing so?

5 Distinguish the style and matter of the arguments put forward by Moloch, Belial and Mammon.

6 How successful is Milton in his presentation of God?

7 How does Milton present the Garden and Adam and Eve *before* the Fall?

8 Illustrate Adam's love for Eve. What part does it play in his fall?

9 What means does Satan employ in his temptation of Eve?

10 Why does Eve fall?

11 Why does Adam fall?

12 What effect does the fall have on Adam and Eve?

13 Discuss Satan as an actor, putting on different parts for different occasions.

14 Is the story a tragedy? To what extent has it a 'happy ending'?

15 How justified is the charge that Milton's verse in *Paradise Lost* has a 'monotonous ritual'?

Paradise Regained

Paradise Regained is a brief epic, in four books. Christ's temptation in the wilderness is seen as a re-enactment of the Fall, in which Satan is resisted.

Book I, lines 1–7 (p.112)

As in *Paradise Lost*, Milton announces his theme. Paradise is to be regained by Christ, the 'greater Man' of Book I of *Paradise Lost*, whose 'firm obedience' will withstand Temptation, in contrast to Adam and Eve, who had yielded to it.

Book I, lines 64–105
Satan addresses his peers (pp.112–13)

Satan undertakes his second great challenge, again involving 'fraud'. Satan sounds not very enthusiastic about his chances of success on his expedition.

page 113

obtains Holds, governs

Book I, lines 290–366
Christ in the wilderness (pp.113–15)

The wilderness is presented as a 'pathless desert', 'by human steps untrod'. It is a gloomy and miserable place in which to find 'our Morning Star'. Satan appears, unexpectedly disguised as an aged rustic gathering sticks. The first temptation is to turn stones into bread. Christ's reply is quiet and simple: 'who brought me hither / Will bring me hence'. As God brought Moses and Elijah out of the desert, 'the same I now'. He makes it clear that he has immediately penetrated Satan's disguise.

page 113

Morning Star The title given to Christ in Revelation

page 114

worm Serpent
an aged man The gospels say nothing about what form the
 Tempter took
caravan A convoy of merchants

Book I, lines 377–405 (p.116)

Satan brings his powers of rhetoric to bear. He asks for pity, presents himself as a reformed character, not half as bad as he's painted. He tries to appeal to Christ's compassion.

attent Attentively

Book II, lines 368–91 (pp.116–17)

Satan has set out a magnificent banquet in front of Christ. Christ replies 'temperately', but with a degree of contempt, that he can produce banquets himself if he has a mind to it.

page 116

What doubts the Son of God Why does the Son of God hesitate?
Defends Forbids

Book II, lines 406–42, 450–67, 481–6 (pp.117–19)

Satan's next temptation is subtler: 'thy heart is set on high designs . . . but wherewith to be achieved?' Christ is unknown, has no followers. What he needs is money. 'They whom I favour thrive in wealth amain, / While virtue, valour, wisdom, sit in want.'

   Christ, still patient, replies that wealth is useless without virtue, valour, wisdom; that the ancient empires dissolved despite their 'flowing wealth'; that some in 'lowest poverty' have achieved 'highest deeds'. The important thing is that a man 'reigns within himself'.

page 118

Antipater the Edomite, / And his son Herod Both
   acquired power because of their riches
puissant Powerful
Gideon and Jephtha and the shepherd lad Gideon, Jephtha
   and David were all poor
Yet not for that a crown Not because a crown

Book IV, lines 43–151 (pp.119–22)

Satan uses all his powers of rhetoric to give a brilliant picture of Roman civilization, Rome 'queen of the earth'. But Rome is now governed by a monster; with Satan's help Christ could govern 'all the world'.

Christ rejects this on the grounds that the riches of Rome are 'luxury', its embassies are 'flattery'; if its Emperor is a devil, that is only because the 'Devil has made him such' and his primary duty is to expel the Devil. Rome is exhausted by 'lust and rapine' and its people have made slaves of themselves. Christ's kingdom, 'on David's throne' will 'overshadow all the earth' and 'of my Kingdom there shall be no end'.

page 120

turms Troops
the Appian road ... the Aemilian The Appian road led south, the Aemilian north.
Syene An Egyptian city
Meroë An island and city in Ethiopia
Bocchus Mauritania
Gades Cadiz
Germans, and Scythians ... to the Tauric pool All Europe from the Danube to the Northern Sea
This Emperor Tiberius
a wicked favourite Sejanus

page 121

citron tables Tables made of citron wood
Setia ... Crete The first two are Italian, the last two are Greek

Book IV, lines 538–80 (pp.122–3)

Satan takes Christ up to a pinnacle of the temple and urges him to stand or throw himself down to be sustained by the angels. Christ stands and it is Satan, defeated, who is cast down, full of

> Ruin and desperation and dismay,
> Who durst so proudly tempt the Son of God.

Both the situation and the language are reminiscent of Satan's first fall from Heaven.

page 122

hippogrif An imaginary creature, part horse, part griffin, on which some of Ariosto's heroes were conveyed about

page 123

Antaeus The son of Neptune and Tellus
Alcides Hercules
that Theban monster The Sphinx. When the riddle was solved by Oedipus, she threw herself into the sea.

Book IV, lines 636–9 (p.123)

Christ 'unobserved / Home to his mother's house private returned'. By this time Milton had come to identify virtue with the private life.

Questions on Paradise Regained

1 In what ways does the style of *Paradise Regained* differ from that of *Paradise Lost*?

2 Discuss the presentation of Christ and Satan in *Paradise Regained*.

Samson Agonistes

Samson Agonistes, in form, is a Greek tragedy. The original story can be found in the Book of Judges. Samson is a great hero who suffers from a fatal flaw: he foolishly trusts a woman who betrays him. The play deals with the last phase of his life, culminating in the moment when, restored to God's favour after much suffering and repentance, during which he slowly learns to resist the temptation to despair, he pulls down the temple on the Philistines and on himself. It takes the form of a series of dialogues with different people who come to visit him in his captivity. There are interpolated soliloquies by Samson, and comments by the Chorus. The verse uses lines of irregular length with irregular rhyme.

Lines 38–59
Samson, captive and blind (p.124)

Samson's self-contempt is forcefully expressed in

> Ask for this great deliverer now, and find him
> Eyeless in Gaza at the mill with slaves.

The divine prediction was that he 'Should Israel from Philistian yoke deliver'. He is tempted to question the divine prediction, not realizing that it will still come true. But Samson has to admit that his captivity is his own fault, since he 'weakly to a woman must reveal' the secret of his strength. His wisdom was unequal to his strength: it was 'hung in his hair' and was easily lost. Behind the self-loathing is a note of self-pity.

secure With a sense of false security
subserve Serve as a subordinate

Lines 80–109 (pp.124–5)

This is a great cry of pain at his blindness. The blank verse breaks down and at the end shrinks to hopelessness. The darkness is a grave; he is his own moving coffin; yet, unlike the dead, he is still able to suffer other pains. The repeated 'dark' is the cry of a strong wild animal beating against a cage from which it can never escape.

silent as the moon 'luna silens' – 'silent moon' – was a Latin
 phrase for the absence of the moon
Hid in her vacant interlunar cave i.e. when there is no moon,
between the old and the new moon

Lines 293–306 (pp.125–6)

The Chorus asserts the justice of God, but perhaps leaves us
more with a sense of the 'perplexities involved'. To 'vindicate
the ways of God to man' was also the purpose of *Paradise Lost*.

ravel Become obscured
still Always

Lines 1623–59
Samson pulls down the theatre (pp.126–7)

A Messenger reports this off-stage event, the climax of the
play. Milton was very good at descriptions of physical viol-
ence and enjoys the 'incredible, stupendious force'. Samson
finds himself again, prays, and puts himself into the hand of
God. In

> those two massy pillars
> With horrible convulsion to and fro
> He tugged, he shook, till down they came and drew
> The whole roof after them

the movement of the lines perfectly embodies the sense. The
massy pillars are *there*; then they begin to rock; the placing
of 'drew' at the end of the line holds the roof momentarily
suspended till it all comes down in a rush. 'Lords, ladies, cap-
tains, counsellors, or priests' are scattered indiscriminately.

reason Reasonable

Lines 1708–24 (p.127)

Manoa's joy that 'Samson hath quit himself / Like Samson' and the Philistines are destroyed speaks for itself. There is a touch of selfish paternal pride (in keeping with the character he shows elsewhere) that Samson has brought 'his father's house eternal fame'. The end is fitting:

> nothing but well and fair,
> And what may quiet us in a death so noble.

sons of Caphtor Philistines

Lines 1745–58 (p.128)

The Chorus reinforces Manoa's thought: 'All is best'; God's wisdom is justified 'in the close'. The end is 'calm of mind, all passion spent'. In his Introduction, Milton had said that tragedy was 'said by Aristotle to be of power by raising pity and fear, or terror, to purge the mind of those and suchlike passions, that is to say to temper and reduce them to just measure with a kind of delight'.

dispose Dispensation
in place By his presence
band them Band together
His servants Manoa and the Chorus
acquist acquisition

Questions on Samson Agonistes

1 Examine the psychological process by which Samson turned defeat into triumph.

2 Like *Paradise Lost*, *Samson Agonistes* is designed to show the Justice of God. Show how Milton achieved this.